PINSTRIPE

Pride

PINSTRIPE

The Inside Story of the New York Yankees

MARTY APPEL

WITH A FOREWORD BY MICHAEL KAY

SIMON & SCHUSTER BOOKS FOR YOUNG READERS
New York • London • Toronto • Sydney • New Delhi

SIMON & SCHUSTER BOOKS FOR YOUNG READERS

An imprint of Simon & Schuster Children's Publishing Division

1230 Avenue of the Americas, New York, New York 10020

Text and compilation copyright © 2012, 2015 by Marty Appel

Adapted for a younger audience from *Pinstripe Empire* copyright © 2012 by Marty Appel

Jacket typography and illustration copyright © 2015 by Luke Lucas

Photos on pages 158, 162, 163, 164, 168, 172, 174, 177, 179, 183, 184, 188, and 197 courtesy Michael Grossbardt

SIMON & SCHUSTER BOOKS FOR YOUNG READERS is a trademark of Simon & Schuster, Inc.

For information about special discounts for bulk purchases, please contact Simon & Schuster Special Sales at 1-866-506-1949 or business@simonandschuster.com.

The Simon & Schuster Speakers Bureau can bring authors to your live event. For more information or to book an event, contact the Simon & Schuster Speakers Bureau at 1-866-248-3049 or visit our website at www.simonspeakers.com.

Book design by Krista Vossen

The text for this book is set in Bembo.

Manufactured in the United States of America

0115 FFG

2 4 6 8 10 9 7 5 3 1

Library of Congress Cataloging-in-Publication Data

Appel, Martin.

Pinstripe pride : the inside story of the New York Yankees / Marty Appel. — First edition.

pages cm

ISBN 978-1-4814-1602-3 (hardcover) — ISBN 978-1-4814-1604-7 (ebook)

1. New York Yankees (Baseball team)—History—Juvenile literature. I. Title.

GV875.N4A665 2015

796.357'64097471—dc23

2014013978

FIRST
EDITION

To the grandparents and parents who pass
along the love of baseball to young fans

Acknowledgments

In tracking New York Yankees history from before the time I became personally involved with the team in the late 1960s, much is dependent on the written words produced by generations of sportswriters in books, magazines, and newspapers. Thank you for those in that profession. You may not have thought you were writing for history, but your work lives on.

On a personal note, thanks to Team Appel—Lourdes, Brian, and Deb—for the continuing support, to my monthly sportswriter luncheon group where nothing is too obscure, and to the fine people who work in professional baseball (majors and minors), whose company and counsel has always been appreciated.

Special thanks to all who first helped and offered encouragement with the original project that led to this book, and a shout-out to young fans Max Perlman, Max Horning, Michael Gross, Ryan Lansing, Matt Nadel, and Guy Lev-Ari, whose input at the start of the project was enormously helpful.

© YES Network

Foreword by Michael Kay

I grew up with a dream that I wanted to play first base for the New York Yankees. That dream ended in a hurry, as I was a rational kid who knew that being afraid of being hit by the baseball was not a good way to make it to the big leagues.

But I made an adjustment. At the age of nine, knowing I was all field, very little hit, I declared to my parents that I was going to be the announcer for the Yankees. Pretty lofty goal for an adult, let alone a nine-year-old. And if you do the math, the inability to a hit a baseball actually decreased my chances to be a part of the Yankees. Consider: A major league team carries twenty-five players on a roster and might add a few more if there are injuries or demotions during the season, while most major league teams have just two play-by-play announcers, one on radio and one on TV. That's it. That means twenty-five to maybe forty men have a chance to play for the Yankees in a season, while two men get the coveted job of calling the action.

With the odds against me, I knew I had to do my homework. I devoured everything I could possibly get my hands on regarding the New York Yankees. I wanted to know everything about this franchise. In school, most every book report I handed in was on a Yankee biography. I read anything I could that had anything to do with the Yankees. I needed to know their history, from the Highlanders to the Yankees, from Jacob Ruppert to George Steinbrenner, who bought the team in 1973, when I was twelve.

To say my parents were a bit concerned with my obsession might be understating matters. Wanting to be the Yankee announcer is a pretty heady goal, and the chances of reaching it were remote, but they never discouraged me. They would occasionally tell me to maybe diversify my interests a bit, just in case I did not get the job, but teachers told them, as long as it gets him to read as much as he does, let him do it.

Boy, could I have saved a lot of time if *Pinstripe Pride* had been around when I was a kid. This book is a veritable primer for any youngster who has a love of the Yankees and a desire to know the history of the organization. Everything is covered. From Babe Ruth to George Steinbrenner, from Lou Gehrig to Derek Jeter, you will get the scoop. And the stories are endless, and interesting, and impossible to put down.

Growing up in the Bronx, my Yankees were Bobby Murcer, Thurman Munson, Ron Blomberg, and Roy White. They were the heart of a team that struggled in the late 1960s and early 1970s. Players like Horace Clarke and Jerry Kenney tried their best but dotted a roster that just wasn't good enough. This stretch of time was one of the rare down times in Yankee history, but for a kid, when the Boss turned things around and put together championship squads in 1977 and 1978, it made it all sweeter. I certainly wasn't spoiled.

In *Pinstripe Pride*, you get a chance to read about all of them, and all of those teams. Players like Bernie Williams, Jorge Posada, Andy Pettitte, and Mariano Rivera come to life as you learn the back stories of what made them great.

I've always felt that connecting the eras of players and sitting down and comparing their stats amounts to a history lesson passed from generation to generation. My dad would tell me about Ruth and DiMaggio, and I would try to imagine what they would be like on the team for which I was rooting. I think love of sports connects mothers and fathers and sons and daughters, all the way back to grandparents. It's a common language spoken through the years that never feels old or dated. The stories you read in *Pinstripe Pride* serve as the thread through the fabric of our lives, uniting all ages within the Yankee mosaic.

For me to have gotten the opportunity to be just a small part of the story when I was hired to broadcast Yankee baseball in 1992 is a small Bronx miracle. A kid who grew up ten minutes from the stadium has had the chance to call World Series championships and perfect games, while being witness to some of the greatest moments in the team's history. Although corny, it is true that sometimes dreams come true.

And with the realization of my dream, I've been fortunate enough to meet some of my idols from childhood and actually call some of them friends. When a thirty-year-old gets to meet Bobby Murcer (the reason I wore number 1 in Little League) and find out he is as fine a man as he was a ballplayer, it brings out the little boy in you.

Pinstripe Pride is a book you will find hard to put down. The guess here is that when your parents say it's time for bed, this is the book that you read under the blanket with the help of a flashlight. And when you're done, you'll probably read it again to see if you missed anything.

Who knows, the next Yankee announcer might be reading this right now, storing all the data in his or her memory to bring up on a future Yankee broadcast.

After covering the Yankees as a newspaper reporter, Michael Kay began broadcasting Yankees baseball in 1992 and is the principal play-by-play announcer for the team's telecasts.

CHAPTER 1

You Can't Make This Stuff Up

If the people who ran baseball could have created a superhero to come and save the day, Babe Ruth would have been their guy.

In appearance, in personality, and in ability, he was almost like a comic-book creation. Even his nicknames—the Babe, the Sultan of Swat, and the Bambino—made him seem like he wasn't real.

But he was real, and his name would have come up over the dinner table at the fancy New York restaurant where the owners of the New York Yankees—Jacob Ruppert Jr. and Til Huston—dined with their friend, Harry Frazee, owner of the Boston Red Sox.

It was Christmastime in 1919. Fans and newspapermen and people who worked in baseball were still talking about the World Series that year, in which the heavily favored Chicago White Sox had lost badly to the underdog Cincinnati Reds. There had been rumors that players on the White Sox might have lost on purpose—bribed by gamblers to "throw" the series. That way, those gamblers could cheat and bet against the White Sox, knowing they would lose, and collect on bets.

It would be another year before the players were arrested for doing just that. They came to be called the Black Sox, and the Black Sox scandal was the worst to ever hit baseball. If gamblers could take over the games by bribing players, then the public trust was gone and the future of the major leagues was in doubt. It was baseball's worst moment since it had become a professional game in 1869.

So of course Ruppert, Huston, and Frazee would be talking about it. Everyone was.

Frazee not only owned the Red Sox, but he also produced Broadway shows and lived on Park Avenue in New York. It was not uncommon for him to socialize with the Yankees owners. Might they have a few beers with their dinner? Of course! Ruppert, after all, was not only co-owner of the Yankees, but owner of the Jacob Ruppert Brewing Company, one of America's largest beer producers.

Babe Ruth was baseball's biggest star from the time he joined the Yankees in 1920. (Rogers Photo Archives)

The Yankees and the Red Sox had just begun making trades with each other. Five months earlier, in July, the Sox sold a suspended pitcher—Carl Mays—to the Yanks, a deal that the league president, Ban Johnson, tried to stop. Johnson said it wasn't right to sell a player, and to reward him with a new contract while he was under suspension. It wound up being decided in court, making the Yanks and the Red Sox allies against Johnson. Johnson lost, Mays became a Yankee, and he won nine games in the final two months of the season.

The Red Sox were the more successful team at this point—they had been to the World Series five times since the American League was founded in 1901. They were playing in an eight-year-old ballpark, Fenway Park, where their "Royal Rooters" were very loud and very supportive.

The Yankees had yet to win a pennant, much to the frustration of their fans and their owners. They didn't even have their own ballpark. They were much less interesting to New York sports fans than the New York Giants baseball team, and the ballpark the Yankees shared with the Giants—the Polo Grounds—was much more crowded when the Giants were playing. Ruppert, in fact, had first tried to buy the Giants before "settling" for the Yankees in 1915, bringing in Huston as a partner.

"So, Harry," Ruppert might have said, "what are you working on these days?"

And Frazee might have responded, "I've got a dandy Broadway musical in the works called *No, No, Nanette*, but I'm still short of funding for it. It's always about raising the money when you're in this business."

"How about your baseball team, Harry? What's going on with the Red Sox?"

"Well, I'd like to get back to the World Series, of course. I think we can do it, and I think we can do it with or without this big lug Ruth. He's such a discipline problem. No rules seem to apply to him. Frankly, he's asking for too much money, and my patience is wearing thin with him."

When it came to training rules, like eating the right foods, getting to sleep on time, and generally staying in shape and behaving himself, Babe was not always a model of perfection.

Babe Ruth. Ruppert and Huston probably glanced at each other, maybe winked. They were baseball men, and they knew all about him. He was becoming the biggest box office attraction in the game and had just moved to the outfield, so his bat could be in the lineup every day. He had always been a pitcher—and a terrific one at that—but the team's manager, Ed Barrow, saw something special there: the ability to hit home runs like nothing that fans had ever seen. Long ones. High ones. Dramatic ones. A lot of them. How could he be doing this, when the baseball itself was considered a "dead ball," incapable of soaring great distances? Hardly anyone was hitting home runs. Maybe eight or ten a year could lead the league, many of them of the inside-the-park variety.

Imagine trying to hit a pillow two hundred feet, if you want to know what the dead ball felt like! You would soon stop trying and learn to hit it a shorter distance, but between fielders.

Ruppert, although born in New York, came from a German family and sometimes spoke with a German accent. He pronounced Ruth as "Root."

"Would you ever consider selling Root?"

"Oh, I might indeed," would have been the response. Frazee was probably already counting the money, realizing he could finance his Broadway productions with it.

This was not a total surprise to Ruppert and Huston. They had earlier dispatched their manager, Miller Huggins, to talk to Frazee, and Huggins had reported that Ruth might be available, perhaps for the huge sum of $125,000.

Ruppert had at first been taken aback by the cost, but he wound up sweetening the deal and making it even more irresistible to Frazee. He would also lend him $300,000, with Frazee putting up Fenway Park as collateral to secure the loan.

Saying "This could be a Merry Christmas for us all," they toasted the deal with another round of Ruppert beer. They would announce it after the New Year. Frazee would be rid of his disciplinary problem, and the Yankees would have a new star to advertise.

He would be the biggest star baseball had ever had. Wait until New York fans got a load of this one, Ruppert and Huston thought. George Herman "Babe" Ruth was going to be a Yankee.

And the history of the Yankees, the history of the Red Sox, and the history of baseball would never be the same.

Ruth had come to baseball from an unlikely beginning. Considered by his parents to be too difficult to handle, he had been placed in St. Mary's Industrial School for Boys in Baltimore when he was only seven. How difficult could he have been at age seven that his parents felt he needed to be placed in a home for unruly boys? In his autobiography, Ruth began by writing, "I was a bad kid."

Really? So bad as to be placed in a home for the next twelve years?

No one ever really understood why he was sent to St. Mary's.

His mother was thought to be ill, either physically or mentally. His father, who owned a saloon, deposited him at St. Mary's in 1904. It must have been frightening for young George, and we know little about visits from his parents, or time away from the home, which also served as an orphanage.

The best thing that happened to him at St. Mary's was meeting a priest named Brother Matthias Boutlier, a six-foot-six-inch Canadian who happened to love baseball. He organized and coached school teams and encouraged George to play. And so the young Ruth first tried out baseball equipment and learned to play the game.

He was a natural. Gloves for lefties were not always easy to find, and large uniforms not always available, but Brother Matthias knew that this was the game that made George feel important, made his life at St. Mary's fun. It even gave him some discipline. At the time, he was mostly a pitcher who threw hard and had good control.

In his twelfth year at the school, he got a lucky break. His skills had been noticed by scouts, and on January 14, 1914, he was offered a contract to pitch for the local minor league team, the Baltimore Orioles. (This was a different team from today's major league team with the same name.) He was placed under the guardianship of Jack Dunn, owner of the Orioles, and someone said, "Oh, that's Ruth, he's just a youngster—he's Jack Dunn's babe." And thus, if we are to believe that story, he became "Babe" Ruth.

He pitched only one year in the minors, winning twenty-two games, dividing his season between Baltimore and Providence, Rhode Island. He even got called up to pitch in five games for the Red Sox, who purchased his contract from Dunn in July. It would be his first of six seasons in Boston, where he helped win two world championships, set pitching records, and became one of the best pitchers in the game.

And yet, his hitting was so good that the Sox needed his bat in the lineup every day. And so on days he didn't pitch, he played the outfield. And in 1919, his last year in Boston, he hit an unheard-of twenty-nine home runs—a new record!—and pretty much wrapped up his pitching career to focus on hitting. On the Yankees he would be an everyday outfielder.

Some people didn't like his style of ball. Baseball had always been played by "building runs"—getting singles and doubles and walks, stealing bases, and coming through with sacrifice bunts. The best players in this style had been Ty Cobb and Honus Wagner, and people who loved baseball loved Cobb and Wagner and the way they played.

The way Ruth played—socking balls over fences and producing one, two, three, or four runs at once on a regular basis—was thought by those older fans to be somehow improper, not the way you play the game. But it didn't take long for everyone to marvel at Ruth's power. How could anyone do this? It was changing everything—attendance, fan interest, and strategy. And Babe was such a colorful character that film footage of him would regularly be featured as part of newsreels in movie theaters—which is how people saw their news in the days before television. If you went to see a silent movie, there would be the Babe, tickling some young tykes, meeting presidents, grinning for the cameras, wearing funny hats, visiting kids in hospitals, and moving his broad body at pretty good speed around the bases. (The newsreels played in fast motion.)

Babe was a perfect character for what came to be known as the Roaring Twenties. The 1920s was a carefree time in America. The Great War (later called World War I) had ended, and Americans were enjoying the feeling of victory and of being an important nation. People were buying cars, roads were being paved, there was radio in the homes, jazz music was cool, and the economy was

If there was a baseball player in an advertisement in the 1920s, it was probably Babe Ruth.
(Marty Appel Collection)

good. There was a law called Prohibition, which made it illegal to manufacture or drink beer, wine, or whiskey, but it didn't seem to bother most people—they found a way to get alcohol. And if you happened to run into Babe Ruth at night, chances were good that it was at a saloon, or a "speakeasy" as they were called, where you could order a drink just like before Prohibition. But you had to be very quiet about it. (Prohibition lasted until 1933.)

America was falling in love with the Bambino. And by the time the Black

Sox players were thrown out of baseball in 1920, people's attention had shifted to the heroics of the Babe. To this day, many people feel that the arrival of Babe Ruth right after the betting scandal probably saved baseball from ruin. Who cared about eight nitwit cheaters in Chicago when people could marvel at the feats of the Mighty Bambino?

He became the idol of every American boy. He made the Yankees into baseball's most glamorous franchise and made every boy want to grow up to wear the Yankee uniform.

Beginning with the Babe's arrival in New York, the Yankees would go on to win twenty-six world championships over the rest of the twentieth century.

Boston won none. None!

Almost a century has passed since he joined the team, but his name remains the best known in baseball history, and he is usually still considered the best player of all time. He was, at once, the best player in the game playing in the biggest city in the country, and stardom was his for the taking. He didn't let the opportunity pass him by.

CHAPTER 2

The American League Comes to New York

Ban Johnson, the American League president, was the Yankees' hero when they began, nearly twenty years before the Babe arrived.

The National League had begun play in 1876. For twenty-five years, they operated with little competition.

Johnson created the American League in 1901, and it was a major league, but it did not have a team in New York, America's biggest city. The American League paid higher salaries than the National League did, and they even managed to steal away some of the National's big stars, like the great pitcher Cy Young, who went to Boston. But Johnson knew that his league wasn't really "big-time" without a team in New York.

The New York Giants were an important part of the National League, and they didn't want the competition from another team in New York. The Giants also had a lot of political friends in New York City, and they relied on their friends in high places to keep Ban Johnson from putting one of his American League teams there by rejecting proposals for new ballparks.

"Can we build a field here?" Johnson would ask.

"Nope."

"How about here?"

"Nope."

"What about here?"

"Sorry."

Without a field, there was no point in creating a team. And so the American League went two seasons without a team in New York.

New York was important to baseball because the game had taken hold there.

Big Bill Devery was co-owner of the original Yankees and tried unsuccessfully to run for mayor of New York.
(Marty Appel Collection)

The fans had been fans for a long time. As early as the 1840s, the game had taken shape on the fields of Hoboken, New Jersey, where volunteer firemen from New York would sail across the Hudson River from Manhattan to enjoy a day off with a bat, a ball, and four bases.

There were popular teams around New York even before there was a National League. The Excelsiors of Brooklyn was the team of Jim Creighton and Candy Cummings, and the team where curveball pitching was invented. In 1882 a league called the American Association included a team in New York called the Metropolitans (Mets, for short). New York baseball fans, called cranks, were in love with the game and happy to support local teams. (This was a different New York Mets from the current National League team, which began in 1962.)

During the 1902 season, the Baltimore Orioles team of the American League went bankrupt. (This was again, not the same Orioles team of today, nor was it the minor league team Babe Ruth played for—but another Baltimore Orioles team altogether.) They were not going to be able to field a team in 1903, and Johnson needed to replace them. Again, he looked to New York, hoping to find potential owners for a new team.

There, a sportswriter named Joe Vila introduced him to two fellows who would be interested in owning a team. One was Frank Farrell, "the Pool Room King," who operated many gambling houses around the city. It was a business that was not legal, but thrived because Farrell paid off corrupt policemen to look the other way.

One of the policemen Farrell paid off was Big Bill Devery, who was the chief of police, but not a very honest one. He was on the receiving end of these payments, he knew Farrell, and he was a person of influence.

Johnson had hoped that his American League would have high standards, well-mannered fans, and no gambling. The National League did not have a good reputation. The fans were rowdy, and it wasn't a good place for women and children to attend. Farrell and Devery didn't meet Johnson's high standards, but because of their connections, they turned out to be the men who could get a ballpark built that the Giants wouldn't stop.

The park would be in an area of northern Manhattan so hilly and undeveloped that the Giants figured no one would bother going there anyway.

And so Farrell and Devery paid $18,000 to own the New York American League team—and then spent about $275,000 to level the land with dynamite, fill in a creek, and build a ballpark. The site was at 165th Street and Broadway, which today is the site of New York-Presbyterian Hospital. The neighborhood is called Washington Heights, and Alex Rodriguez was born in that neighborhood many years later. Some of the apartment buildings that were across the street from the ballpark, and that can be seen in old photographs, are still standing today.

Fans have come to think of the team by the nickname "Highlanders," and the ballpark as "Hilltop Park." Actually, at the time the team played there, they were usually just called the New York Americans, and the signs at the park just said AMERICAN LEAGUE PARK. Newspapers had trouble getting "Highlanders" into

Hilltop Park, first home of the Yankees (then called Highlanders), as depicted in this painting by William Feldman. (GoodSportsArt.com; copyright William Feldman)

headlines and, on their own, began to use "Yankees" or "Yanks" as early as 1904. Fans who went to the hilltop would have to take a streetcar up Broadway. Starting in 1905, they could take the new subway and get off at the Polo Grounds—where the Giants played—and walk ten blocks uptown. By 1906, they finally had their own subway stop.

The ballpark was made of wood, as were most ballparks of the time. And most of them eventually caught fire and burned down. Hilltop Park served as home to the Highlanders for ten years and never burned down. (In fact, it was the better-constructed Polo Grounds that had a big fire in 1911, and they had to share Hilltop Park for a few weeks while the damage was repaired.)

And so the Yankees were born in 1903, the year the Wright Brothers made the first flight, and the year a baby named Lou Gehrig was born just a couple of miles away. The Yankees would learn more of him about twenty years later.

While Hilltop Park wasn't fancy, it was actually a nice place to see a game. The park could hold about sixteen thousand people, and if you were sitting in the higher seats along the first-base side, you had a terrific view of the setting sun over the Hudson River and the New Jersey Palisades, a line of steep cliffs that run along the river. It was a peaceful setting to enjoy the game, buy a hot dog, keep score with a pencil and a simple scorecard, and enjoy visiting players like Ty Cobb, Walter Johnson, Cy Young, and Nap Lajoie when they came to town.

Except maybe for the day in 1912 that Cobb went into the stands to beat up a fan who was heckling him. Cobb had a sour personality, and his temper was well known. But going into the stands was beyond anything that could be tolerated. Ban Johnson suspended him for that, and his Detroit Tigers teammates, in support, refused to play the next day. Rather than forfeit the game, the Tigers signed up amateur players from local sandlot teams and lost 24–2. And although they only played a single game, all those amateur players are forever listed in record books as having played for the Detroit Tigers.

Ban Johnson (some modern historians like to call him BanJo) wanted the New York team to be good, so he helped Farrell and Devery where he could. He helped get Clark Griffith, a very respected and aging pitcher, to be the manager. The two best players to join the new team were pitcher Jack Chesbro and outfielder "Wee Willie" Keeler.

Chesbro was a good pitcher in the National League but became a great one in New York. In the Highlanders' second season, 1904, he won forty-one games.

That is more than the number of starts today's pitchers make, so for the time being, it is safe to assume no one will ever break that record.

Chesbro's best pitch was a spitball, a pitch that broke almost uncontrollably when a pitcher covered the ball with saliva mixed with tobacco juice. The Highlanders had many pitchers who used that pitch. It was legal until 1920, when it was finally banned for being unsanitary—gross, actually—and giving pitchers an unfair advantage. (We now know that chewing tobacco is a health hazard as well.) The owners in 1920 wanted more home runs hit, and fewer

"Wee Willie" Keeler could "hit 'em where they ain't"—and that is how he answered a question about his success. (Rogers Photo Archives)

weapons for pitchers to get the hitters out. Pitchers who relied on it were allowed to continue to throw it until they retired (this is called "grandfathering" a rule). The last one of these, Burleigh Grimes, did so in 1933.

Keeler had a lifetime .371 average during his twelve years in the National League, including a forty-four-game hitting streak and a .424 average in 1897. He was only five foot four and 140 pounds, and the Highlanders gave him a $10,000 contract, which made him the highest-paid player in the game. He came from Brooklyn, so he was a popular local player, but when he stood in right field in Hilltop Park on opening day in 1903, the fans couldn't help but laugh. Right field hadn't been fully seeded with grass yet, and Keeler kept getting stuck in the mud. To keep him from sinking into it, the team had to bring out wooden planks for him to stand on.

Occasionally during the years in Hilltop Park, characters joined the team and won the fans' hearts. The scrappy little infielder Norm "the Tabasco Kid" Elberfeld was popular, and the first baseman, Hal Chase, was not only popular but the best fielding first baseman of his time. Unfortunately, Chase was often suspected of betting on games, and there were things about his play that made people wonder if he might be losing on purpose to win bets. One of his teammates said, "I always wondered why he would often be just a step late in taking throws at first base!"

Generally speaking, though, the years in Hilltop Park were not very successful ones. The team wasn't very good, nor was it all that interesting. Home runs? This was not their style, and at the time, it wasn't how baseball was typically played. In fact, between 1904 and 1910, only eight over-the-fence home runs were hit at Hilltop Park.

The closest they ever came to a championship was in 1904, their second season. The pennant race came right down to the final days of the season, and it was between New York and Boston, the first important contest between two teams that would form one of the great rivalries in sports.

Trainloads of Royal Rooters (a Boston fan club) came from Boston for the big final series. As bad luck would have it, Chesbro, trying for his forty-second win, threw a wild pitch over the catcher's head, allowing Boston to win the game and the pennant. The pitch was probably a spitball that got away. The sportswriter Mark Roth, who was credited with first calling the team "Yankees," reported that Chesbro was crying on the team's bench after the game. Players took winning and losing just as seriously then as they do today.

"Prince Hal" Chase, shown here in a Giants uniform, was popular with the fans, but players thought he was often gambling on the outcome of his games. (Rogers Photo Archives)

CHAPTER 3

Not Much Luck, Not Any Pennants

After Griffith left as the team's first manager in 1908, there were a lot of managers who tried but failed to make the team successful. Even players Elberfeld and Chase had their turns. So did Frank Chance, a first baseman who'd won four pennants with the Cubs as manager, but who couldn't find success in New York. (Chance was famous because a poem was written about the Cubs' infielders turning a double play, and it was popularly known as "Tinker to Evers to Chance.")

A man named George Stallings took a turn as manager and failed. Although he later led the Braves from last place on July 4 to the 1914 National League pennant and came to be called a miracle worker, he wasn't one in New York.

During this time, the Highlanders uniform seemed to change every year. But a cap with the NY logo that we know today emerged in that period. The design was first seen on a police medal designed by Tiffany, the famous jeweler, and the team adopted it as their logo. Occasionally the team wore pinstripe uniforms. Years later people said the pinstripes were designed to make Babe Ruth look slimmer. But that wasn't the case—they were used before he got there.

A very controversial issue at the time for all teams was playing games on Sunday. Sunday was the only day off for many working-class people. But because many of the nation's laws were influenced by church teachings, it was illegal to charge admission and encourage fans to go to baseball games on the Sabbath. Politicians who supported teams playing Sunday games were scolded during church sermons. Yet Sunday was the day teams could get their biggest crowds, so it was very tough for the owners to lose that income.

The argument raged on for years. It wasn't until 1919 that Sunday baseball was permitted in New York, as politicians finally voted to lift the ban. In some cities the ban lasted even longer.

Among the politicians who supported Sunday baseball was a New Yorker who happened to be president of the United States. Teddy Roosevelt was a baseball fan, and in 1908 he invited the team to the White House for a visit. Looking back, we can see how big baseball was becoming: During the visit, the president told the players that his ten-year old son Quentin, who was at school,

Frank Farrell (elbow out) was co-owner with Bill Devery of the original Yankees. Here he occupies a box seat at the Polo Grounds, after the Yankees moved there in 1913. (Bain News Service)

would be "inconsolable" at missing a chance to meet the players, because he "worshipped them and knew all of their records."

After the 1912 season, another losing one for the Highlanders, the team decided to move out of Hilltop Park. They would make a deal with the Giants to share the Polo Grounds, paying rent to the Giants for their seventy-seven home games. The feuding between the two rivals had simmered down, especially after the Giants had accepted an offer to share Hilltop Park after their fire. Now the Polo Grounds had been rebuilt into the finest park in the land.

CHAPTER 4

The Highlanders Become the Yankees

Make no mistake about it, the Giants were still the most popular team in town. They had Christy Mathewson as their big star. He was admired by all for his intelligence and gentlemanly manners, in addition to his great pitching skills.

The Yankees—they were no longer called the Highlanders—had no big stars and offered little hope. The Giants drew more fans, made more money, and created more excitement. The Yankees—well, they just sort of existed. Their 1913 team not only finished last, they hit only eight home runs and averaged fewer than five thousand fans a game. As Yogi Berra once said, "If people don't want to go to the games, you can't stop them."

Ban Johnson's patience with the Yankees had grown thin. Farrell and Devery simply weren't providing the good New York team he had hoped for.

And after 1914, they agreed to sell the team to Jacob Ruppert and Til Huston, the owners who would eventually acquire Babe Ruth.

Ruppert was the better known of the two. Since the Ruppert Brewery employed so many people, since he had been a congressman from New York, and since Ruppert beer advertising was all over town, everyone was familiar with the Ruppert name.

He was called Colonel Ruppert by many, but it was more an honorary title than a military rank, coming from an executive position with the New York National Guard.

Young Jacob Ruppert inherited his father's brewery and purchased the Yankees with Til Huston in 1915.
(Rogers Photo Archives)

Ruppert was very rich. He had a mansion on Fifth Avenue and a country estate in Garrison, New York. He owned racehorses and yachts, bred Saint Bernards, had collections of rare books, jade, and porcelain, and kept a collection of monkeys at his estate! He was a member of important country clubs, helped finance exploration missions, wore the finest suits, and employed butlers, maids, and chauffeurs. Being seen at a ballpark might not have been the style of his fellow country club members, but he loved baseball.

The Colonel could certainly have bought the Yankees by himself—the price was $460,000—but he wanted a partner who also had good political connections. The partner was not as refined as Ruppert, despite his rather fancy name of Tillinghast L'Hommedieu Huston—"Til" for short. Huston, who was in the military, was sometimes called Cap, and sometimes also Colonel, which were ranks he had reached in the service. He had made his money developing land in Cuba after the Spanish-American War, and in the family business of railroad development.

Ban Johnson was still the powerful president of the league, and to help induce Ruppert and Huston, he had promised to help them acquire some star players for the Yankees. The problem was, he had made the same promise to the new owner of the Cleveland Indians.

When the Boston Red Sox decided to make their star center fielder Tris Speaker available, Johnson had a problem. Speaker was exactly the sort of player who could turn a ball club into a winner. A terrific fielder and a terrific hitter, he would for many years be mentioned with Ruth and Cobb as part of the "all-time greatest outfield."

Speaker wound up with the Indians. Ruppert never forgot what he thought was Johnson going back on his word.

The Yankees did get some good new players, however. One, the pitcher Bob Shawkey, came from the Philadelphia Athletics and would go on to become the team's winningest pitcher by the time he retired. Another, Wally Pipp, was a big man for his time and a good first baseman. Another, to play third base, was Frank "Home Run" Baker. While enjoying his best seasons with the Athletics, Baker got his nickname by hitting some clutch home runs against the Giants in earlier World Series. Although Baker is the only player ever nicknamed "Home Run," he hit only ninety-three in his career, and twelve was his high mark for any one season.

Ruppert and Huston selected an old pitcher, Wild Bill Donovan, to be the Yankees' new manager. Donovan had twice been a twenty-five-game winner as a pitcher but was now pretty much retired. He replaced Roger Peckinpaugh, who had managed the team in 1914 at the age of twenty-three. Peck is still the youngest manager in baseball history. He was also the team's shortstop, and with no hard feelings, went back to just being the shortstop and captain when Donovan was hired.

Donovan was popular with the writers (he had pitched for Brooklyn, and they all knew him in New York), and no one doubted that he had a good baseball mind. But as with all his predecessors, the lack of stars doomed the Yankees to the middle of the standings. There were occasional big moments, like on April 24, 1917, when a pitcher named George Mogridge pitched the first no-hitter in Yankee history. Mogridge was a pretty ordinary pitcher on other days, but on that day he became the only visiting left-hander in history to throw a no-hitter in Fenway Park. In fact, only three other visiting pitchers have ever done it, all right-handers, and they are all in the Hall of Fame—Walter Johnson, Ted Lyons, and Jim Bunning. So it was no small accomplishment, coming in the fifth season of Fenway Park history. (Fenway Park is now over one hundred years old.)

Now the question for the Yankee owners was whether to keep Donovan or move on.

CHAPTER 5

Enter Miller Huggins

Huston was impatient with Donovan after three seasons, and his preference was the Brooklyn manager, Wilbert Robinson. But Huston was far away and didn't have the clout to make his position felt. He couldn't text his thoughts to Ruppert. He couldn't phone them. He almost couldn't mail them.

Where was Huston? He was in Europe. World War I had broken out, and he was back in uniform, far from baseball. In Huston's absence, Ruppert replaced Donovan for the 1918 season and signed the Cincinnati manager, Miller Huggins.

Huggins, a former infielder, was only five foot five and weighed about 120 pounds soaking wet. To be a successful manager he had to have shown great character and great leadership skills, for athletes tended to respect physically bigger managers and to take advantage of the smaller ones. Babe Ruth would be one of the worst offenders in this way—and Huggins would never be able to control the Babe. But that would come later. For now, he was being hired to run the 1918 team, in what would turn out to be a season with a shortened schedule, due to the war and the call-up of many players to fight. The season ended on Labor Day, and fourteen Yankees entered the service. The team finished fourth, in the middle of the pack once again, but Huggins would come back in 1919, assuming the war was over and baseball was resuming.

Miller Huggins became manager of the Yankees in 1918—and, three years later, won the team's first pennant. (Rogers Photo Archives)

One player of this era who drove his managers crazy was a pitcher named Ray "Slim" Caldwell. Ray had a bad drinking problem, and although he was a talented player, managers never knew if he was going to show up for games. Frequently he would be suspended for his bad habits.

In 1918, after nine seasons in New York, the team had enough and traded him to Boston. He had won ninety-six games for the Yankees—second only to Chesbro—but he was now considered more trouble than he was worth.

The adventures of Slim Caldwell didn't end there. The following year he was with Cleveland. In his very first start, leading with two outs in the ninth inning, he was struck by lightning and knocked unconscious while on the mound.

"My first thought was that I was through for all time," he recalled. "Living as well as pitching. But when I looked up and saw I was still in the diamond and fans were in the stands, just as they were before I was hit, I just had to laugh with joy. I never was so glad to be living in all my life, and wouldn't it have been tough luck for me to be stricken just as I had won my first game for a club that was willing to give me a chance. I tingled all over and just naturally sank to the ground."

He finished the game with a victory. And seventeen days later, he faced his old teammates, the Yankees, and threw a no-hitter against them.

The *New York Times* wrote, "If [the fans] hadn't been there in person, many of them would never have believed it . . . a lot of the electricity is still lurking in Caldwell's system."

Ray Caldwell was struck by lightning and, two weeks later, no-hit his old Yankee teammates. (Rogers Photo Archives)

In 1919 the Yankees got Carl Mays from Boston, and after he arrived, the team played well and finished a position better in third, drawing their highest attendance to date (over six hundred thousand for the season) and making Huggins look good, perhaps even to Huston.

The year 1919 was, of course, the year of the Black Sox scandal. And then came Babe Ruth. The Yankees wouldn't have to worry about being middle-of-the-road much longer.

CHAPTER 6

Here Comes the Babe

In a sense, Yankee history was about to begin. The first two decades had been listless and unrewarding. Managers came and went, big stars were nowhere to be seen, and the Giants ruled the town. The Yankees talked about having their own ballpark one day, but for now, they remained tenants of the Giants in the Polo Grounds, and not very interesting to follow on a daily basis. Huggins was a fine fellow, but John McGraw, the Giants' manager, well, he was the toast of the town. When he had dinner at a restaurant, every newspaper wanted to report on it.

But Babe Ruth was about to change all that. He was about to make everyone sit on the edge of their seats whenever he came to bat. No one could look away. He was easy to spot because of his size and moon face, and he would always give the fans a show. Even when he struck out—which he did more than anyone—he was exciting.

And as it happened, he loved the Polo Grounds. The right-field foul line was only 258 feet away, and that was Ruth territory. As a left-hand hitter, that was his target. And he found it often.

In Ruth's first season with the Yankees, 1920, he proved to be worth every nickel that Ruppert and Huston had forked over for him. In 1919 at Boston he had slugged those twenty-nine home runs for a new record. In 1920 with the Yankees, he hit fifty-four, and a year later upped it to fifty-nine! No wonder the fans were going crazy watching the big guy. He was doing things never before done. It was unimaginable!

The year he hit fifty-four, it was more than every other team in the league hit. Babe's slugging percentages in those two seasons were .847 and .846. (Slugging percentage is figured by dividing total bases by at bats.) No one really knew what a slugging percentage was before Babe came along—a new statistic entered the game, just for him.

Babe Ruth loved hitting in the Polo Grounds with its short right-field foul pole.
(GoodSportsArt.com; copyright Bill Purdom)

Despite Ruth, the Yanks still finished third—but they did win ninety-five games and were only three games out of first. They were genuine pennant contenders and quickly becoming the glamour franchise in the league.

The 1920 Yankees drew 1,289,422, marking the first time that a team had ever drawn a million. They outdrew the Giants for the first time.

The Giants were suddenly anxious for the Yankees to find a new home of their own. They didn't want to be embarrassed as New York fell in love with the Bambino.

CHAPTER 7

Carl Mays Beans Chappie

Despite all the joy of suddenly being a hot team with a big drawing card in Ruth, there was a bad moment in 1920 that would rock the baseball world. Sadly, it happened in a Yankees game at the Polo Grounds.

The Cleveland Indians had come to town. It was Monday, August 16, and they were in first place, with Speaker as their center fielder and manager, and shortstop Ray Chapman their most popular player and on-field leader. Indians fans called him "Chappie," and for many young fans in Cleveland, he was the Man.

Games started at three p.m. then, so it was around four p.m. when Chappie came to bat in the fifth inning. On the mound for the Yankees was Carl Mays, their ace. As popular as Chappie was in baseball, that was how unpopular Mays was. He just had a sour personality and not many friends.

But no matter, he was good. He was known for throwing a hard underhand "submarine pitch," and that's what he fired at Chappie.

The ball struck Chapman around his ear. Some thought the sound, and the result, might have been caused by a bunt, for he did raise his bat as though to try a running bunt.

But Chapman, stunned, did not run to first, even though he had been hit by the pitch. Mays fielded the ball and threw to Wally Pipp at first, thinking he was recording an out.

Chapman fell to the ground. The umpire called for a doctor, and one came down from the stands. Finally he got to his feet and, with the help of his teammates, walked to the Indians dugout. There he collapsed.

Submarine pitcher Carl Mays hit Cleveland's Ray Chapman in the head in 1920, long before players wore helmets. (Rogers Photo Archives)

He was taken to a nearby hospital and was reported to be in "grave condition." Poor Chappie died early the next morning. It was the only time that a major leaguer had been killed in a game. A helmet might have saved him, but players would not wear helmets for many years.

Mays was taken to a police station the next day, but he was never charged, and it was considered nothing more than a horrible accident. Needless to say, he did not accompany the team to Cleveland on their remaining trips there, fearful of the fan reaction. His lack of popularity in baseball did not help. In fact, players on four other teams threatened to strike if Mays wasn't thrown out of baseball. He wasn't thrown out, but for the rest of his career he was usually booed by fans on the road. Some felt he was worthy of consideration for the Hall of Fame based on his career record, but voters would have none of it.

Although the spitball had been banned that very year, the Chapman death resulted in other changes to the game. It was head trauma that had caused his death, and baseball officials moved quickly to make the ball easier to see. From then on, clean baseballs would always be used by pitchers, the better to be seen by batters. No more worn, scuffed, dirty baseballs would be in play. It might cost the team more money to supply more baseballs, but it was considered a necessary step. (Today it is common to use as many as one hundred baseballs in a game.)

You would think the accident would cause baseball to consider the use of helmets. It wouldn't have been a new invention; helmets were worn by soldiers in World War I. Manufacturers could certainly make them. But baseball is slow to change. It took fifty-four years after the invention of instant replay to allow umpires to use it to get calls right. It took forty-three years after a famous home plate collision involving Pete Rose and Ray Fosse in an All-Star Game for the major leagues to ban dangerous home plate collisions. It would be some thirty-five years before players regularly wore helmets. It was a long time coming.

After the incident, the Indians went on to win the 1920 World Series, "winning it for Chappie," they said.

By now, only the Yankees, the Washington Senators, and the St. Louis Browns had yet to win an American League pennant.

The Yankees' turn was coming.

CHAPTER 8

Pennants and a New Ballpark

With Carl Mays leading the pitchers and the Babe belting his fifty-nine home runs, the 1921 pennant was the Yankees' first. After all this time, the win was very sweet indeed. It was their eighteenth season, the seventh year that Ruppert and Huston had owned the team, and the fourth season with Hug as manager. Only one player from the Highlander years—pitcher Jack Quinn, who had returned to the team in a trade—was able to enjoy the triumph.

The Yanks also won the pennant in 1922, and they played the Giants in both the 1921 and 1922 World Series. Since the Yanks and Giants shared one ballpark, this meant all World Series games for those two years were in the Polo Grounds, taking turns being the home team.

For many fans, standing in the streets looking at big public scoreboards was the way to way to follow the World Series. These scoreboards, hanging outside newspaper offices, kept fans posted, batter by batter. And the fans, packed closely together in anticipation, would ooh and aah at every crucial pitch.

Unfortunately for the Yankees, Ruth had an injured left elbow and missed most of the 1921 Series. The Yanks lost, though perhaps they would have won if Ruth had been healthy. As it was, the losing players each received $3,510—a lot of money in the days when their full-season salaries could be as low as $5,000.

The 1922 World Series was the first one broadcast live on radio, but again the Giants won, the Yankees managing only a tie in one game. (Before lights were installed in ballparks in the 1930s to enable night games, there were a lot of ties due to darkness.)

This would be the end of the Yankees' days in the Polo Grounds. The Giants had asked them to find a new home, which was fine with Ruppert. He felt that his team, now of championship caliber, deserved its own place, and he had been looking around for some time. And so he bought out his partner, Huston, and purchased land just across the Harlem River from the Polo Grounds to build his own ballpark.

Carl Mays pitching to a packed house at the Polo Grounds in the 1922 World Series.
(New York Public Library)

He called it Yankee Stadium.

You could see one park from the other, but this would mark the move of the Yankees to the borough of the Bronx. (New York comprises five boroughs, including Brooklyn, where the Dodgers played.)

The area that would be Yankee Stadium was cleared, and a remarkable ballpark was built in only 284 working days. Twice the word "stadium" had been used in baseball—once in Washington, where National Park changed its name to Griffith Stadium in 1920, and once at the Polo Grounds, where John Brush, the owner, tried to change it to Brush Stadium. The newspapers and the fans kept calling it the Polo Grounds, though. (College football had used the term

Aerial photo of Yankee Stadium shortly before it opened in 1923. (Marty Appel Collection)

"stadium" since Harvard Stadium opened in 1903.) But Yankee Stadium was the first baseball field that truly deserved such a grand word.

Ruppert could have called his park Ruppert Stadium, which would have helped advertise his beer, but this was a time in the United States when Prohibition was in force, and the sale of beer (or any alcoholic product) was illegal. The ballpark held more than sixty thousand people (almost double what most ballparks at the time held), it had three decks, and there were plans in place to run the capacity up to almost eighty thousand. (That never happened, but the park was expanded twice, first in 1928, then in 1936, when the triple decks were extended into the original bleacher areas.) For many years, people would say, "the Yankee Stadium," but eventually it was just "Yankee Stadium."

A sportswriter, Fred Lieb, nicknamed it "the House That Ruth Built," a tribute to Ruth making the Yankees a championship team and propelling its need for a bigger ballpark in the first place.

It was also built to Ruth's liking, because the right-field foul pole was only 257 feet from home plate, which made an easy target for Ruth, a left-hand hitter. In its second year, the distance to right became 294, which was still a very inviting distance for Babe.

Center field, however, was an enormous distance away—490 feet!—so far

Artist depiction of Yankee Stadium in 1923. (David Kramer, Matt O'Connor, J. E. Fullerton, Michael Hagan, Scott Weber, Michael Rudolpf, Dennis Concepcion, and Chris Campbell)

that a flagpole was placed in deep center field because no one could hit the ball that far. (Eventually it was reduced to 457, but the flagpole remained.) Left center field would settle in at 402, making it a real challenge to bat right-handed and play in Yankee Stadium.

The most interesting-looking portion of Yankee Stadium was the copper frieze (or facade) that hung down from the roof around the field. The design gave Yankee Stadium a look of great majesty, and players were in awe at being circled by three decks and that royal frieze. When the stadium was remodeled in 1976, the frieze was removed (except for over the bleacher billboards), but when the new stadium opened in 2009, it was back, circling the park and restoring that grandeur. Visiting players, especially rookies, would look up and say, "NOW I feel like I'm in the big leagues!"

Opening day of Yankee Stadium was April 18, 1923. The record attendance in baseball history to that point was 42,620, for a 1916 World Series game in Boston. On this day, a reported 74,200 fans made their way to the Bronx to see history. And to their total delight, Ruth hit the first home run in the House That Ruth Built, and the Yankees won 4–1 against the Red Sox.

No one cheered louder than Little Ray Kelly. He was the Babe's personal mascot. For eleven years, starting when he was only three years old, he would be in the Yankee dugout, cheering for the Babe. Babe had seen him having a catch with his dad in Riverside Park, in the neighborhood where Ruth lived, and "adopted" him for this job. He would pick him up and drive him home. They posed for pictures together. Sometimes Babe even took him on road trips, promising Ray's parents to look after him.

Did his teammates resent that Babe had his own mascot in the dugout and no one else did?

"Are you kidding?" answered Ray, when he was an adult. "He was Babe Ruth! He could do whatever he wanted! And he was helping those teammates earn a lot of World Series money!"

Little Ray Kelly was discovered playing catch with his dad, and Babe Ruth adopted him as his mascot, often posing for photos with him. This was opening day of the new Yankee Stadium in 1923. (Ray Kelly)

Little Ray had one special job at home games. The team kept an ice chest in the dugout. Ray's job was to make sure there was a cabbage in there so that Babe could peel off a leaf each inning and put it under his cap to keep his head cool. No one else was allowed to take a leaf from Babe's cabbage.

CHAPTER 9

The Game Has Changed

If fans today could go back in a time machine to the time that Babe Ruth played, they would recognize the game immediately, because the rules and the field measurements have not changed much. But a lot *has* changed over the years.

For one thing, the players were not as big then as they are today. Today's players use trainers, work out in gyms, and are better educated about the right things to eat. Their clubhouse meals are healthier. Since the players make a lot more money today, they don't have to take jobs in the winter and can devote more time to staying in shape.

Almost every position has become a "hitter's position." For a long time, infielders were expected to be good fielders, but not especially good hitters. Today, infielders are expected to hold their own in the lineup and hit the ball well.

Scouting today is more scientific. The use of video to study opponents and computers to record every pitch results in fielders knowing better where to stand for each batter, and pitchers knowing better how to pitch to each hitter (and vice versa). In the old days, managers relied on memory to know how to position fielders against hitters. Pitchers and catchers relied on memory for each batter, too. Of course, in those old days, they played each opposing team twenty-two times. That was a big help in learning the habits of opponents. Today, some opponents are seen as few as six times a year.

The fields didn't look as good as they do today. Groundskeepers have learned how to keep the grass looking good all season, and players aren't spitting tobacco juice on it as they used to. In the old days, by the end of the season there would be a lot of bare patches. The infields are also better cared for. It wasn't unusual to have pebbles create bad hops (unexpected, errant bounces) on old infields—today it almost never happens. The Yankees even lost a World Series—in 1960—when on the Pittsburgh infield a ball hit a pebble, which took a bad hop into their shortstop's throat!

Some fields even have artificial grass, especially ones in indoor ballparks, where grass couldn't grow. The first indoor ballpark was built in 1965 in Houston, Texas, and featured "Astroturf." The Yankees have always played their home games outdoors on natural grass, but of course, some of their road games came to be played on "turf."

In the early days of baseball, uniforms were made of heavy flannel and were baggy. Since the 1960s they have been tailored to fit tighter and make the players look faster and stronger. Since the 1970s uniforms have been made of a cooler knit material. Today's players also wear protective helmets and batting gloves. That didn't used to be the case. (Jorge Posada, who was said to be "old school," never wore batting gloves.)

In the American League, today's game has a designated hitter to bat instead of the pitcher. That provides more hitting in the game; pitchers were usually easy outs who never paid much attention to their hitting. The "DH" came along in 1973, although the National League chose not to use it and still sends its pitchers up to bat.

The role of the pitcher has changed over time too. Until the 1960s, starting pitchers were expected to pitch complete games. Only on occasion was a relief pitcher important enough to a team to become a star. By the 1980s, teams were using "closers" to finish games, and the complete game was as rare as a shutout used to be. No one kept track of pitch counts before the eighties, and it was possible that some pitchers might throw as many as two hundred pitches a game. Today most pitchers have a limit of 100 to 110, and then they come out.

Players in the old days traveled by train, slept overnight in Pullman sleeper cars, and played only day games until lights started to appear on ballpark roofs in the 1930s. Yankee Stadium didn't have lights until 1946. All the major league teams were located in the northeast quarter of the United States—no farther west than St. Louis, Missouri, no farther south than Washington, DC, or Cincinnati, Ohio. Plane travel made it possible to expand to the West Coast in 1958, when the Brooklyn Dodgers and New York Giants moved to Los Angeles and San Francisco.

If one looks at a team photo of any team from before 1947, only white players appear. That was because baseball followed an unwritten rule that black players—and dark-skinned Hispanic players—could not play. Much of America was segregated like that. When that barricade finally came down, the quality of the overall talent in the game immediately improved. Baseball was slow to open the gates to black players—but actually faster than other industries or schools in America were.

While the game's biggest stars could earn nice salaries, most of the players made about the same as the average working man. Not until the 1970s were players permitted to offer their services to a team that might pay them more money. This development, called free agency, made a lot of players into millionaires. But before that, you had to stay with the team that had you under contract, even when the season and the contract ended.

Kids going to games—mostly boys until the 1970s—would make scrapbooks of their favorite players and wait outside the ballparks to get autographs in their autograph books. They joined fan clubs. They chanted "We wanna hit! We wanna hit!" when their team was at bat, and "We want an out! We want an out!"

when they were in the field. Fans used to dress up for games, often in jackets and ties, usually wearing hats. Today's fans are much more casual, although many wear team caps and T-shirts, including T-shirts with the names and numbers of their favorite players.

In the old days, a fan could buy a hot dog, a soda, peanuts, popcorn, and Cracker Jack at the ballpark. Today a wide variety of food is sold. For souvenirs, fans used to be able to buy a pennant, a team badge with a player's photo, and a scorecard. Starting in the 1950s, a team yearbook was added. Today's fans can choose from hundreds of souvenir items in team stores not only in the park, but at stores in the cities and online.

One of the fun parts of being a fan today is catching a foul ball. Since the 1990s, players are also encouraged by major league baseball to toss balls to fans whenever they catch a third out and retrieve a foul. The balls cost only about ten dollars each for the team, and the fans get a terrific thrill out of going home with a game-used baseball. But it wasn't always that way. Until the early 1920s, fans were asked to throw the balls back so that they could continue to be used. It wasn't until 1921, when a Polo Grounds fan who refused to return one actually sued for the right to keep it, that baseball relented and allowed the fans to keep the balls.

At a ballpark today, the scoreboard is part of the show, along with the music played over the public address system. There was a time when the scoreboard showed nothing but the score! There was no public address system until the 1940s. And there was no music in the ballparks until the 1950s and 1960s. Men with megaphones would walk around near the stands and holler out lineup changes to the fans.

Following baseball used to mean reading the newspapers. There were more than a dozen daily newspapers in New York, available at the turn of the century for as little as a penny, and kids read them for the comics and the sports. Starting in the 1920s, fans could follow baseball on the radio. Television came along in the 1940s. Color television became popular in the 1970s. Today the Internet adds even more ways to follow baseball and for people to create their own blogs to talk about the team to their own followers. And players can tweet messages directly to fans through their own Twitter accounts.

The coming of pocket calculators in the 1970s and personal computers in the 1980s allowed fans who really loved their statistics to become even more involved. New statistics were developed. It seemed like almost everything except "number of cracked bats" was recorded.

Years ago, fans read the *Sporting News* each week. All fans, young and old, could recite batting averages, and maybe how many games pitchers had won. Home runs were not an important statistic, because there weren't many. They were like triples are today—people didn't especially remember the number that each player hit. Much has changed, but Babe Ruth would have been a big star in any era.

CHAPTER 10

Lou Gehrig Arrives

The year 1923 saw the debut of a very special Yankee rookie named Lou Gehrig.

Gehrig was born in New York City the year the Highlanders were born, 1903, about halfway between Hilltop Park and the future site of Yankee Stadium. He was an only child, and whereas Ruth's parents pretty much abandoned him, Gehrig's doted on him, watching his every move. He was so close with his parents, he lived with them until he got married at age thirty. While Babe was forever getting himself into trouble, Lou never seemed to do anything wrong. As a player, he was held up as a hero to boys everywhere. (Girls hadn't yet become big baseball fans.)

Gehrig's parents were German immigrants and wanted Lou to have a fine education. They enrolled him at Columbia University, where he tried out for the baseball team. He was special. When the Yankees scout, Paul Krichell, went to see him play a game at Rutgers University in New Jersey, he called his boss, Ed Barrow (the Yankees' bushy-eyebrowed general manager), and said, "I saw another Ruth today." (The general manager handles the signing of players, while the manager handles the on-field game.)

Lou Gehrig was a role model for youngsters all over America for his clean living and hard work.
(Rogers Photo Archives)

Krichell signed Gehrig to a Yankee contract, and Lou played his first game for the Yanks on June 15, 1923. He played only twelve more games that year and hit his first home run. Wally Pipp was the Yankees' first baseman, and a good one. Lou would have to wait for his chance at first base to show what he had. Krichell was confident that day would come soon.

It came on June 2, 1925. Pipp complained to Huggins that he had a headache, and Hug gave him the day off. He put Gehrig at first base.

The Pipp headache became a symbol to all workers in sports and elsewhere, that if you take a day off, you never know if your job will still be there when you return. Gehrig stayed at first the next day, and the next . . . and the next. Pipp's headache was better, but he wasn't in the lineup. The new guy was too good. Pipp got traded.

For the next fourteen years, Lou never missed a game. Not one. He would go on to play 2,130 consecutive games. The previous record had been 1,307, held by Everett Scott, who happened to be a Yankee teammate at the time Lou's streak began.

Gehrig had to be lucky to be able to play every day. He had no broken bones and no illness that kept him bedridden. He became an American symbol of hard work and the rewards it would bring.

For years people thought this would be the most unbreakable record in baseball. But there is an old baseball saying, "Records are made to be broken," something even Babe Ruth would experience. Gehrig's record was broken in 1995 by the Baltimore Orioles' Cal Ripken, who would go on to play 2,632 in a row. Gehrig's record held for fifty-six years after he retired. Now it is said that Ripken's record will never fall.

We'll see.

Gehrig had huge muscles compared to other players of his era. He was incredibly strong, and while his home run totals were not as high as Ruth's, he was clearly the second-best slugger in the game. No one came close to those two for a long time.

Ruth typically batted third in the lineup, and Gehrig fourth. What a one-two punch they were! The entire Yankee lineup in the 1920s, though, was so good it could drive pitchers crazy. The lineup came to be called "Murderers' Row," because of how they would "murder" their opponents time after time.

With Babe Ruth hitting .393 (a Yankee team record to this day), the Yanks won their third straight pennant in 1923—and once again, they faced the Giants.

The first World Series home run ever hit in Yankee Stadium was a thrilling, inside-the-park home run by Giants outfielder Casey Stengel, who thought he lost a shoe while running furiously around the bases, yelling out loud to himself, "Go Casey go, go Casey go!"

It was really just a small sponge inside his shoe that flew out, and when he slid home in a cloud of dust, he told the next batter, Hank Gowdy, that he'd lost a shoe.

Gowdy said, "How many were you wearing, Casey? You have two on!"

But the lost shoe became part of Casey's growing legend, and twenty-six years later, he would take that legend to the Yankees, where he would become a very successful manager.

The Yankees were leading the World Series three games to two, and had a 6–4 lead going into the eighth inning of game six. They were six outs away from the title. "Sad Sam" Jones was the Yankee pitcher, and he set down the final six batters.

Finally the Yankees were able to beat the Giants in a World Series. On October 15, 1923, in the Polo Grounds, the Yankees could be called world champions for the first time. It was their twenty-first season. It was their first year playing in Yankee Stadium.

In the clubhouse, Ruth jumped on a table and said, "Boys, we've won the world championship, and we owe a lot of the accomplishment to the guiding hand of Mr. Huggins. He has done a great job this year in managing the team, and we want to present you with this ring in token of the esteem in which we hold you."

Babe must have been so sure of victory that he had purchased a ring in advance. Throughout their time together, Babe usually drove Huggins crazy with his bad behavior, his rule breaking, his late nights out, and his lack of discipline. Occasionally he would make up for it with big gestures like this. What a fine moment this was for Hug.

Each player received a gold watch in addition to their $6,143 World Series check. (The first World Series rings were awarded in 1922 to the Giants; the first time the Yankee players got rings was 1927.) There would be many days of triumph to come in Yankee history, but this one had been a long time coming, and the first is always special.

"Three cheers for Huggins," shouted the players. "Hip hip hooray!"

The Yankees didn't win the pennant in either 1924 or 1925, and 1925 in particular was just an awful year, with the team finishing in seventh place. And Babe was the focus of the trouble.

The year began with him suffering what was called "the bellyache heard round the world," an illness he got near the end of spring training, when he collapsed at the railroad station while the team was heading north, playing exhibition games against the Dodgers at many stops along the way. (This was the first year in which the Yankees had spring training in St. Petersburg, Florida—a practice which continued, except for wartime and 1951, until 1961.)

They got Babe to a hospital in New York, where he lingered into May, and he didn't play his first game until June. Then he got into a dispute with Huggins late in August over staying out late in St. Louis after a 1–0 loss. Tensions were already high between Ruth and Hug, and this time, Huggins suspended Babe and fined him five thousand dollars—an enormous sum.

Ruth left St. Louis and went right to New York, where he intended to talk his way out of the suspension and fine directly with Colonel Ruppert. But Ruppert supported his manager. After nine days, Huggins restored Ruth to the team, hoping he had learned his lesson.

Ruth's "bellyache" and later suspension were national news. Without that bad season, the Yankees would have gone forty-six straight years—until 1965—without finishing in the lower half of the standings, known as the second division. Instead they finished in seventh place.

But the team quickly rebuilt in 1926, adding a shortstop, Mark Koenig, and a second baseman, Tony Lazzeri. Lazzeri was the first in a line of great Italian-Americans signed by the team, a line that would come to include Joe DiMaggio, Phil Rizzuto, and Yogi Berra. Lazzeri was a tough kid with little formal education, and he had considered being a boxer before turning to baseball.

In the minor leagues, he had hit sixty home runs for Salt Lake City (the league played a very long season of some two hundred games), attracting great attention.

Lazzeri suffered from epilepsy, an illness that could occasionally cause convulsions and could even be life-threatening in a severe case.

His seizures did not happen often, and teammates seldom witnessed such an episode. No one recalled Lazzeri having a seizure during a game. There was a story of it happening once at the team's hotel. Koenig, his roommate, ran out and got pitcher Waite Hoyt to save him. Hoyt had no real medical background but worked in the off-season as an assistant in a funeral home. The Yankees trainer, who was always with the team, was on another floor of the hotel, and Hoyt's was the door that Koenig chose to knock on.

The Yankees returned to the World Series in 1926, the first Series ever for the St. Louis Cardinals, and Ruth hit three home runs in the third game, two of them said to be over five hundred feet!

This game proved especially memorable because earlier Ruth had responded to a request to send recovery wishes to Johnny Sylvester, an eleven-year-old boy, in his New Jersey home. He promised to "knock a homer for you" on one of the balls he signed for little Johnny.

*Babe Ruth's bedside visit to seriously ill Little Johnny Sylvester in 1926 was said to help in the boy's recovery. The whole nation followed the story. (*New York Daily News*)*

There was a lot of publicity about the promise, and then Babe hit three homers. The story became part of the Babe's legend, and twenty-two years later, when Ruth was dying, Johnny Sylvester visited *him* in the hospital. Sylvester had recovered, and his name would forever be linked to the Babe's.

The World Series ended with high drama a few days later. It was now game seven, and the Cardinals were winning 3–2 in the seventh inning. The bases were loaded for Tony Lazzeri, the rookie second baseman. What a moment!

The Cardinals' manager called for a veteran pitcher, Grover Cleveland Alexander, to come in and face Lazzeri. Alexander, one of the great pitchers in baseball, was not prepared to pitch in the game, let alone come in at such a crucial moment. He was, in fact, not feeling too well, having been out late the night before, sure that he wouldn't get into the game.

In this big World Series moment, though, Alexander came through where it mattered, striking out Lazzeri to save the Cardinals' lead. It became one of the most talked-about at bats in World Series history.

In the ninth inning, with Alexander still pitching and two outs, Babe Ruth walked. He would be the tying run if the Yankees could bring him around, as the Yanks still trailed 3–2.

On the first pitch to the next Yankee batter, Ruth took off, trying to steal second base.

This was not a smart play. You never want a game to end getting thrown out stealing. Babe was a smart runner, but not a speedster. He wasn't known for base stealing.

Sure enough, he was out! The World Series ended with Babe caught stealing. It was an embarrassing moment for Ruth and for the Yankees, as the Cardinals celebrated on the field with a world championship.

"I thought Alex was sleeping out there, and I thought I could get a good jump on him," said Babe.

It didn't work out, and the Yankees lost the 1926 World Series.

CHAPTER 11

Murderers' Row

The 1926 World Series loss led to 1927 becoming one of the team's best years ever. Not only did they win the pennant by nineteen games, winning 110 in the process, but they did it using only twenty-five players. They didn't make a single roster change all season.

Joe Judge, a player for Washington, spoke for almost every opposing player when he said, "Those fellows not only beat you, but they tear your heart out."

The entire decade of 1920s Yankee baseball is considered legendary, but the '27 team stands out. Any argument today about "best team ever" usually begins with the 1927 Yankees. (It also includes the Yankees of 1939, 1961, and 1998.)

Besides Ruth, Gehrig, Lazzeri, and Koenig, there was Jumping Joe Dugan at third (he got his nickname because he "jumped" from team to team early in his career), Earle Combs and Bob Meusel in the outfield, and a pitching staff headed by Waite Hoyt, Herb Pennock, Urban Shocker, and Bob Shawkey. (There was no single star catcher; three men shared the position.)

The 1927 Yankees also had a twenty-sixth man in their team photo—but he was an imposter! And he managed to get into the team photo of what would be considered the greatest team in history.

His name was Don Miller. He was never on the team, but he just hung around the Yankees a lot, sometimes wearing a uniform and pitching some batting practice. On the day of the team photo, someone must have yelled, "Hey, Don, get in here!" And he did. He stood next to Babe Ruth, and he even signed his name when everyone autographed the picture. It is one of the great imposter stories of all time!

1927 NEW YORK YANKEES
WORLD CHAMPIONS

Front Row — JULIE WERA, MIKE GAZELLA, PAT COLLINS, EDDIE BENNETT (mascot), BENNY BENGOUGH, RAY MOREHART, MYLES THOMAS, CEDRIC DURST.
Middle Row — URBAN SHOCKER, JOE DUGAN, EARLE COMBS, CHARLIE O'LEARY (Coach), MILLER HUGGINS (Manager), ART FLETCHER (Coach), MARK KOENIG, DUTCH RUETHER, JOHNNY GRABOWSKI, GEORGE PIPGRAS.
Back Row — LOU GEHRIG, HERB PENNOCK, TONY LAZZERI, WILEY MOORE, BABE RUTH, DON MILLER, BOB MEUSEL, BOB SHAWKEY, WAITE HOYT, JOE GIARD, BEN PASCHAL, (Unknown), DOC WOOD (Trainer).

The great 1927 New York Yankees team, with "imposter" Don Miller sneaking into the photo, next to Babe Ruth—sixth from left, top row. (New York Yankees)

But the team's *real* players were running away with the pennant that season, and attention shifted to whether Ruth might break his record of fifty-nine home runs. He needed seventeen in the month of September, but he had a mighty month, and sure enough, on the next-to-last day of the season, he clobbered number sixty off Washington's Tom Zachary.

"Sixty!" Babe said in the clubhouse after the game. "Let's see someone try to top that one!"

For thirty-four years, it was the most famous record in sports.

In the 1927 World Series against Pittsburgh, it was said that the Pirates got scared of the Yankees just watching them take batting practice before the first game. And while that is probably an exaggeration, the Yankees won that World Series in four straight, assuring that the '27 Yankees would always be held in the highest regard.

The Yankees won the World Series again in 1928, but there was mystery clouding the season. What was wrong with their pitcher, Urban Shocker? He had been one of their starters on the great '27 team, but teammates knew that something was up.

"He sleeps standing up," they whispered, having observed him on overnight train travel across the country. Before airline travel came along, teams always traveled by train. They really got to form close friendships, played cards together in private cars (sometimes in their underwear!), ate in the dining car together, and talked a lot of baseball. It was a special part of being a ballplayer. (Back then, trains weren't air-conditioned, so that created memorable trips in terrible heat too!)

Shocker didn't exactly "sleep standing up," but he did recline to nearly a full sitting-up position in his Pullman sleeping car. "A four-pillow guy," was what he was, a term for how high he had to prop himself up in bed to avoid putting stress on his heart.

It seemed that Urban was suffering from an enlarged heart, but he never spoke about it. And in 1928, with his illness still a secret, he engaged in a salary dispute with the Yankees and never reported to spring training. In fact, he didn't turn up until Memorial Day, when he pitched just two innings in relief. That would be his last game.

The Yankees released him on July 6, and he went on his own to Denver for medical care, admitting at last that he was going to be treated for what he called his "bum heart."

The treatments didn't work, and poor Urban Shocker died on September 9 after developing pneumonia. He was only thirty-eight.

His funeral was in his hometown of St. Louis, and his family waited a full week until the Yankees were scheduled to be there so that they could attend.

No one felt worse than Huggins, who had questioned Shocker's holdout early in the season and said some tough things about him.

Just a few weeks after being in St. Louis for Shocker's funeral, the Yankees faced the Cardinals once again in the 1928 World Series. The series was pure Yankee power on display. Once again, Alexander was with the Cards, and Lazzeri with the Yankees. Was it going to be a chance for revenge for the 1926 series? After all, fans were still talking about the day Alex struck out Tony in the '26 Fall Classic.

The opportunity for revenge came in the final game of the Series. What a game it was for New York, as Ruth belted three home runs and Gehrig hit his fourth home run of the Series. And then, in the seventh inning, in came Alexander to face Lazzeri. Alexander was now forty-one (he still had two more seasons in him). This time Lazzeri hit a double as part of a four-run inning, which sealed the championship. Sweet revenge!

The players awarded a share of the World Series prize money to the widow of Urban Shocker.

The 1928 Yankees featured a new face—a tall and strong catcher named Bill Dickey. He was what people would call the "strong, silent type." He had a "presence"—he was a leadership sort of player who brought great skills with him.

Dickey came from Arkansas, and would, at age twenty-two, become the team's regular catcher. For thirteen years in a row, he would catch more than a hundred games—a very durable record at a position so injury prone.

Up until Dickey's arrival, the team had not had a top-rated catcher. (We could say "all-star catcher," but All-Star Games didn't start until 1933.) They had gotten by with some good defensive ones, but none who could also hit as well as Dickey could. Bill would be a lifetime .313 hitter and a Hall of Famer, and by the time he retired, many thought he was the best catcher baseball had ever seen.

Everyone liked Bill, but if challenged, he could land a punch and hold his own with anyone. One day in 1932, Dickey's fourth year as a regular, a Washington player named Carl Reynolds slid into him hard at home plate. Dickey felt the slide was out of line and proceeded to break Reynolds's jaw with a hard punch. People were shocked to see him do such a thing, and he wound up suspended for a month. But it was a message to all opponents: You don't mess with Bill Dickey.

By 1929 the "Murderers' Row" Yankees were known across the land with their big stadium, big sluggers, and championships. They had won six pennants in the twenties, a happy time in America—the Roaring Twenties—when people were feeling good about their country and good about their lives. The Yankees were stars, just like silent film movie actors were stars.

The team took to wearing uniform numbers that year—they were the first team to do that. It was Jake Ruppert's idea, and he borrowed the concept from football.

The funny thing was, the Yankees announced they would wear numbers on their backs, so the Cleveland Indians decided to do it as well. And on opening day, the Yankees were rained out, so the Indians were actually the first. But it was a Yankee idea, and they are still known as the team that created it.

The numbers were assigned based on the lineup, which seldom changed. Scorecards were printed in advance, with the lineups included. Earle Combs was the leadoff hitter, and he had number 1. Mark Koenig batted second and wore 2. The Babe batted third and wore 3. Lou Gehrig, the cleanup hitter, was 4, and so on. Number 7, which would one day become famous as Mickey Mantle's number, was first worn that year by Leo Durocher, an infielder on the team who would go on to be a Hall of Fame manager. (Ruth didn't like Durocher, who he was convinced stole Babe's watch out of his locker.)

Numbers on players caught on so quickly that all teams were doing it by 1931. Often, the first thing a fan would think about when talking about a particular player was his number. It was something that set him apart.

The first four numbers retired by the Yankees were 4 (Lou Gehrig), 3 (Babe Ruth), 5 (Joe DiMaggio), and 7 (Mickey Mantle), shown here in Yankee Stadium. (Marty Appel Collection)

CHAPTER 12

Good-bye to Hug

The Yankees did not win the pennant in 1929 (nor in 1930 or 1931), as the Philadelphia Athletics (who today play in Oakland), had assembled a terrific team that proved to be even better than the Yankees at that time.

But two important events took place late in '29.

In late September, with the season nearly done, Miller Huggins developed a serious skin infection called erysipelas. Today that illness is treated with penicillin, which came into use after World War II and was called the "wonder drug." For Hug, they could only treat him with a heat lamp, which proved to be useless. He stayed behind in New York while the Yankees took the train to Boston, and he was admitted to the hospital.

On September 25, while the Yankees were playing in Fenway Park, the American flag was suddenly lowered to half-staff. There was no announcement. The players and fans wondered why. Two innings later, the Yankee team was called together in the dugout and told the news: Miller Huggins had died. All the players from both the Yankees and the Red Sox were called to gather at home plate, where they removed their caps, as the Red Sox public address announcer, using his megaphone, informed everyone of Huggins's death.

Babe Ruth was shaken. He had never treated Hug especially well, and sometimes he had made the manager's life miserable, breaking all his training rules and not taking his leadership seriously. But now, all Ruth could say, his eyes wet from tears, was, "He was my friend. He was a great guy, and I got a kick out of doing things that would help him. I am sorry he couldn't win the last pennant he tried for. We will miss him more every day."

Poor Hug was only fifty-one. For his funeral, the team, now in Washington, took a train to New York, then went back to Washington for their game. Ruth, Gehrig, Lazzeri, Combs, and pitcher Herb Pennock were among the pallbearers. Burial was in Hug's hometown of Cincinnati, and Pennock, who was not scheduled to pitch for several days, went along as representative of the players.

Three years later the Yankees dedicated a monument to Hug out by the flagpole in Yankee Stadium's deep center field. They copied the idea from the Giants, who had a monument for a player named Eddie Grant, who had died in World War I. The Huggins monument would become the first of what would eventually become Monument Park, one of the most sacred areas of any ballpark in America. The number of monuments there eventually grew to five, along with many plaques on the wall honoring special members of the team. Eventually Gehrig, Ruth, DiMaggio, and Mantle had monuments that matched the one for Huggins.

"I guess I'll miss him more than anyone," said Gehrig when Huggins passed away. "Next to my father and mother, he was the best friend a boy could have. He told me I was the rawest, most awkward rookie that ever came into baseball. He taught me everything I know."

CHAPTER 13

Enter Joe McCarthy

A month after the season ended, the stock market crashed. With an unexpected jolt, America went from the Roaring Twenties to the Great Depression. People who'd once had good jobs stood on bread lines or sold apples in the street. The nation was about to go into a decade of great struggle in which money would be very tight. Just as the Yankees—and baseball—were looking forward to continued growth, people had to struggle to come up with twenty-five cents to sit in the bleachers at a ballgame.

Baseball never stopped throughout the 1930s, but it didn't grow much in this era either. In some cities, it wasn't unusual to play before one or two thousand people on a weekday. Jacob Ruppert was lucky—he didn't lose his money in the stock market, and he remained a very wealthy man. He could continue to keep the team going and pay his players. But it was hard to keep going when so many fans were struggling, and when the other teams in the league were just getting by.

It wasn't an easy time for baseball or for the nation. The sport was, however, a great boost to the spirits of the country and provided a little relief from the woes of the time.

Meanwhile, Ruppert had to pick a manager to replace Huggins, and Babe Ruth wanted the job. It was not unusual for star players to become player-managers. Ty Cobb did it, as did many others. For owners, it was actually a chance to save some money by not paying a full salary to a manager.

But Ruppert considered Ruth an unlikely manager. "He can't even manage himself!" he told his friends. Babe was not happy when the job went to his old teammate Bob Shawkey, a longtime Yankees pitching star who had retired three years earlier.

When the Yankees finished third to the Athletics in 1930, Ruppert decided to make another change to the manager position. Again Ruth said he wanted the job, but again Ruppert declined to give it to him. Instead he reached out to Joe McCarthy, who had led the Cubs to the National League pennant in 1929.

McCarthy proved to be a smart pick by Ruppert. A no-nonsense leader with a great mind for baseball, he quickly established hard-and-fast rules for the team and enforced them with great seriousness. He wanted the team to act and look first-class in every way. He made sure they were outfitted with three sets of uniforms, always dry-cleaned, always quickly repaired. While many teams would use the same uniforms in doubleheaders, the Yankees always changed into fresh, clean uniforms between games. They wore suits and ties when traveling. They conducted themselves as gentlemen. Well, almost all of them did. Babe followed his own rules.

McCarthy got lucky in his first season by acquiring two pitchers who would wind up in the Hall of Fame. One had red hair and was named Red Ruffing, and the other threw left-handed and was named Lefty Gomez.

Nicknames or no nicknames, Babe Ruth never remembered anyone's name anyway. He called most people "kid." Ruffing—who had such an easy nickname because of his hair—well, Babe called him Meathead.

Gomez, who came from Rodeo, California, was raised on a dirt-poor ranch, and his tall, thin body gave the impression that he missed a lot of meals. He weighed only about 160 pounds, but he could really throw hard. He had a very good sense of humor, and even when he was a rookie, he could tease his teammates and make everyone feel good. He became great friends with Ruth. Sportswriters took to calling him Goofy Gomez, or El Goofo.

General Manager Ed Barrow (left) signing Joe McCarthy to manage the Yankees. (Rogers Photo Archives)

Because his father, Coyote Gomez, was born in Spain, Lefty had a Spanish last name and was really the first Hispanic star on the Yankees. Today most Hispanic players in baseball come from Latin America, but Gomez could certainly be considered the first great Hispanic Yankee, even if he had European ancestry, and even if he couldn't speak Spanish.

Ruffing didn't have Gomez's sense of humor, and in fact was a no-nonsense, tough customer. He often had contract disputes with the Yankees, and because he was also a terrific hitter, he wanted extra money for his hitting. (One year he batted .374.)

Ruffing started his career with the Boston Red Sox but did not have a lot of success there. In fact, when the Yankees made a trade for him, his lifetime record was a terrible thirty-nine wins and ninety-six losses. No one would have thought he was going to wind up in the Hall of Fame one day.

But he wound up winning 231 games for the Yankees between 1930 and 1946. He won twenty games four times, and he won seven and lost only two in World Series competition. On August 5, 1939, he passed Shawkey as the winningest right-hander in Yankee history, and in 2014, seventy-five years later, he still had that honor. His 231 wins were the most by any Yankee until left-handed Whitey Ford passed him in the 1960s. But it is safe to say that he will remain the winningest Yankee right-hander for many, many years to come.

CHAPTER 14

The Called Shot

McCarthy didn't win the pennant in 1931, but he did in 1932. That season, the Yankees won sixty-two of their seventy-seven home games, which pretty much set the pattern for much of McCarthy's managing career. He always won nearly 70 percent of his home games at Yankee Stadium. And with Babe Ruth hitting a home run once every eight times at bat during his Yankee years (not counting walks), if a fan went to a Yankee home game in those days, there was a very good chance that he could go home and tell his friends, "The Yankees won, and I saw Babe hit a homer!"

But Ruth's most famous home run came in the 1932 World Series.

The Yankees were in Wrigley Field playing the Chicago Cubs, and Charlie Root was pitching. (This was a coincidence, because Ruppert called Ruth "Root" with his German accent.) So it was Ruth against Root in the third game (or Root against Root if you were the Colonel), which was full of World Series frenzy before the excited Chicago fans. This was the team McCarthy had managed before coming to New York!

On the Cubs was the Yanks' old shortstop Mark Koenig. The Yankees thought the Cubs had been cheap to their old friend: They'd agreed to give him only a one-half share of the 1932 World Series money, because he'd joined the team late in the season, on August 5. (Yankee players were loyal, even to their former players.) The Cubs players were heckling Ruth about his age, and bad feelings were in the air.

The Yanks won the first two games, and now, game three was in Chicago. New York governor Franklin D. Roosevelt and New York mayor Fiorello LaGuardia were both there. Babe even paid for his old mascot, Little Ray, to come out to Chicago with his dad for the games.

Artist William Feldman's depiction of Babe Ruth "calling his home run" in the 1932 World Series at Wrigley Field. (GoodSportsArt.com; copyright William Feldman)

Ruth came to bat in the fifth inning with the score tied 4–4. He had already hit a home run in the first inning, and the crowd was really giving him a hard time. Some fans were throwing lemons onto the field in the Babe's direction.

Babe didn't swing at the first pitch from Root, and the umpire called it strike one. The fans were booing and howling, and suddenly Babe raised the index finger of his right hand and pointed straight out.

Was he pointing at the bleachers? Was he suggesting that he was going to hit the next one out? Was he pointing at Root? The catcher, Gabby Hartnett, thought he heard Ruth say something like, "It only takes one."

After two balls, the next pitch was again a called strike. And again, Babe pointed. What was he saying? What did it mean? He had only pointed after strikes.

The next pitch was baseball history. Ruth gave it a mighty swing, and out the ball soared, nearly five hundred feet, deep into the bleachers. Oh, what a moment it was!

This came to be known as the "called shot" home run. Even those on the field that day disputed what they had just seen. A home movie, taken by a fan and released many years later, indeed showed Babe pointing—but to what? The bleachers? The pitcher? The Cubs bench?

It was never really known for sure. Babe was such a great showman, and he knew what a grand moment this was, that he never disputed that he had "called" the home run. "The good Lord was with me that day," he would say.

Gehrig, the next batter, also homered. This seemed like Lou's fate, always performing in the shadow of his great teammate. In light of Babe's memorable moment, few would remember that Gehrig also homered.

Of all the incredible legends of Babe Ruth, this one might be the biggest. It was his fifteenth and last World Series home run and his most famous.

The Yankees won the Series in four straight, with Gehrig batting .529 and hitting three home runs. Of course, Ruth's famous home run overshadowed Gehrig's performance, as usual.

CHAPTER 15

Babe Moves On

Ruth's flair for the dramatic didn't end in 1932, even though he was getting older and nearing the end. The first All-Star Game was played the following year—in Chicago, at Comiskey Park—and Babe hit the first All-Star Game home run.

But the Yankees didn't win the pennant in 1933 or 1934, and Babe's friends kept telling him he was getting a lousy deal, not being allowed to manage. And so after the 1934 season, the Babe departed. Bitter over not being given his chance to manage, and clearly seeing his playing skills diminish, Ruth was ready to go. Ruppert and Ruth both agreed to end Babe's days with the Yankees. Babe would be a player and "assistant manager" with the Boston Braves in 1935, and he felt that there was an understanding that he would eventually manage that team.

He was no longer the great player he had been. But he had one more big day in him. Playing for the Braves in Pittsburgh on May 25, 1935, he hit not one, not two, but three home runs in one game, giving him 714 for his career. And that was it. A few days later, he retired for good. What a way to go out!

Babe never did become a manager. He coached one season for the Brooklyn Dodgers, but otherwise traveled the country as one of the most famous Americans, endorsing products, making appearances, and signing more baseballs than anyone could believe. Today Babe Ruth autographed balls are worth a lot of money, but the truth was, he signed more than anyone else, making them very plentiful. The problem was, no one knew that autographs would ever be worth money. So many times someone would go home with a signed Ruth ball and play catch with it until the signature faded.

It was time for the Yankees to move forward, and to try to find the next Babe Ruth, if that was possible.

CHAPTER 16

The DiMaggio Years

With Babe having left, Gehrig had center stage to himself in 1935, but 1936 brought with it one of the most highly anticipated rookies the game had ever known: Joe DiMaggio.

Joe was born into a large family near San Francisco, where his father earned a living as a fisherman. Three of the brothers became major league baseball players, and all were thrilled to be able to "play a game" for a living instead of taking on the daily hard work of a fisherman. Joe hated the way his dad would come home from work smelling of fish.

Joe was the most talented of the brothers, and right out of high school, he began playing in the highly regarded Pacific Coast League for the local San Francisco Seals. The Seals were considered the high minor leagues, and DiMaggio was able to compete at this level even at eighteen. In fact, he batted .340 at eighteen, .341 at nineteen, and .398 at twenty for the Seals, and in that first year, he had at least one hit in sixty-one consecutive games. No one before or since has ever done that as a professional. There was no hiding this prospect—everyone knew about him.

But in May 1934, Joe stepped awkwardly out of a taxi and tore some bone cartilage in his knee. Suddenly a lot of teams lost interest.

But not the Yankees. They had two scouts on the West Coast—Bill Essick and Joe Devine—whose opinions were highly valued back home in New York. Essick took Joe for a medical examination, and the doctor said he should recover just fine. And on the strength of that, the Yankees bought Joe from San Francisco for $25,000 and five minor league players. He would remain in San Francisco for 1935 as Yankee property, and then he would come to New York.

All eyes were on this young, thin rookie as he joined the nation's most successful team. (Starting with Joe's rookie season of 1936, the team added an "NY" logo to the front of their uniform jerseys—something Babe Ruth had never worn.)

To many, Joe was the perfect baseball player. They call such athletes "five-tool players"—players who could hit, hit for power, run, field, and throw. In no area of the game was he weak. If anything, being a right-handed hitter robbed him of some power in Yankee Stadium, where the left-field stands were very far off. But despite that disadvantage, he was always among the league leaders in batting average, runs, RBIs, and home runs.

He played the game with great style. It was said that he never made a mistake on the field. He always wanted to give the fans his best. "Someone may be seeing me for the first time," he said. "I can't ever loaf."

To Italian Americans, he was a great national hero. Italians formed a large segment of the immigrant population of America, and they were largely working-class people. DiMaggio's accomplishments gave them all a sense of great pride.

"I used to like to just watch him shave," said his teammate Phil Rizzuto, another Italian American who joined the team a few years later.

His teammates respected and admired DiMaggio and valued him for his greatness right from the start. They did not give Rookie of the Year awards in the 1930s (that did not begin until 1947), but Joe had one of the greatest rookie seasons ever. He missed the first month of the season due to a spring training mishap, but he batted .323 with 206 hits in only 138 games.

He became the first rookie to play in the All-Star Game and went on to play every inning of every All-Star Game in his first seven years.

And oh, how he led the Yankees to new greatness in those years! The team won the World Series in every one of his first four years—then just missed winning the pennant in 1940, and proceeded to win three more pennants in 1941 through 1943. Had they won in 1940 (they finished three games out of first), they would have had eight straight pennants. It was almost unthinkable!

Joe, of course, had a great manager in McCarthy, and great teammates, led by Lou Gehrig. Gehrig was happy to have a teammate as fine as Joe, and he did not mind being "back in the shadow" as he had been when Babe Ruth was there. (Meanwhile, Lou was playing every day, and his record of consecutive games played was running up near two thousand.)

The difference was that without Ruth, the team was now a team of great discipline. They went about their business in a very professional manner, carrying themselves with class and distinction and dignity. This came from above—owner Jacob Ruppert, general manager Ed Barrow, and manager McCarthy—but players like Gehrig, DiMaggio, and Bill Dickey set the example of how a Yankee behaved.

Yankee Stadium was kept in very clean condition, making it a pleasant visiting experience for fans. This was still the Great Depression in the United States; not every team could afford proper stadium upkeep and maintenance, but the Yankees could, and their ballpark was the shining jewel of the country's "national pastime."

This was really the time that the Yankees became an institution representing excellence—a reputation that remains today. McCarthy, Gehrig, Dickey, and DiMaggio made sure the Yankees continued winning pennants and world championships, just as the team had done in Ruth's era, and the team set in motion a business plan that seemed to say that this team would always go out and get new stars, and would always compete at a high level. The Yankees as a dynasty seemed to be in good hands.

One of the key players for the Yankees throughout the 1930s was a relief pitcher named Johnny Murphy. Born in New York and educated at Fordham University, he was unusual for his time in that he became a star as a reliever. Until that time, with rare exceptions, relief pitchers were never stars. There was no "save" statistic, and starting pitchers were expected to pitch complete games. Relief pitchers were usually pitchers not good enough to start, and forced to pitch out of the bull pen.

Not so with Murphy. He was very talented and became very popular, and Lefty Gomez would humorously come to thank "Johnny Murphy and a fast outfield" for all his success. For his twelve years in relief for the Yankees, Murphy was a fan favorite. And he was the first in a long line of great Yankee relievers (who eventually came to be called "closers")—going from Murphy to Joe Page to Ryne Duren to Luis Arroyo to Sparky Lyle to Goose Gossage to Dave Righetti to Mariano Rivera. Murphy helped to make the role of closer into a "glamour" position.

The Yankees won four World Series in a row—in DiMaggio's first four years with the team. He must have thought, *This isn't hard at all!*

But by the fourth year, 1939, things were starting to change.

Colonel Ruppert died in January. He left the team in the hands of Ed Barrow, his general manager. Barrow was widely respected as the best in the business, but he was not an easy man to talk contracts with.

Phil Rizzuto took one look at Barrow's eyebrows—the bushiest he had ever seen—and said, "They were ferocious! I couldn't negotiate with someone who looked that stern!"

Another thing that came out of Ruppert's final illness was that the Yankees could now be heard on the radio.

Like the owners of the Giants and Dodgers, Ruppert feared that if you put the games on the radio so people could listen for free, they might not buy tickets to the games. (This same fear was even greater when television came along about ten years later.)

Ruppert was too ill to attend the 1938 World Series. He stayed at home in his mansion on Fifth Avenue and listened to announcer Mel Allen on radio, since the World Series games *were* broadcast. And he liked what he heard. He came to realize that by showing how exciting the games were, and by using radio to talk about upcoming games, you could actually use it to sell more tickets.

And so he instructed Barrow to set up a radio contract, and the Yankees hired Mel Allen to be their broadcaster. He was only twenty-six years old.

Mel had an easy southern accent, knew the game, and had a gift for creative nicknames. DiMaggio was "the Yankee Clipper." Tommy Henrich became "Old Reliable." Late-inning rallies were called "Five O'Clock Lightning." Sometimes he called the team "the Bronx Bombers" when they were really slugging the ball.

Mel would become the "Voice of the Yankees," and people who grew up with radio and later television would learn the game from Mel, and often become Yankee fans because of Mel. People who rooted against the Yankees hated the sound of his voice, of course, because good things always seemed to be happening for the Yanks when they heard it.

Broadcaster Mel Allen nicknamed Tommy Henrich "Old Reliable" for his clutch hitting.
(Rogers Photo Archives)

CHAPTER 17

Farewell to the Iron Horse

Mel's first season, 1939, would be memorable not only because it meant another world championship, but also because something was wrong with the captain, Lou Gehrig. (Gehrig had been named captain—the on-field leader—in 1935.)

Lou had struggled in spring training after his average had fallen below .300 the year before. Maybe he was just getting old. But at thirty-six, he wasn't *that* old, and he was still "the Iron Horse," the man who never missed a game. The streak was still going.

He really played poorly in April. Joe McCarthy would not sit him down, would not end his playing streak. That would be up to Lou. He deserved that respect.

On April 30 at Yankee Stadium, he played his 2,130th game in a row. But he went 0 for 4 to drop his average to .143. He had managed only four singles in April.

The team took the train to Detroit for their next series, but in the hotel lobby, Lou saw McCarthy and asked if he could speak to him in his room. The men went upstairs.

"I'm just not helping the team," said Lou. "I don't know what it is; I just don't feel right. I think it's time to take me out of the lineup."

Both men knew that this was a very big story. The streak was over. Nearly fourteen years without missing a game.

At the ballpark the next day, word spread quickly that Babe Dahlgren would be at first base, not Lou. The Detroit fans knew they were seeing history. Amazingly, Wally Pipp, who Lou had replaced in 1925, lived near Detroit and was at the game that day.

Lou Gehrig never played again. He stayed with the team but slipped away for a few days for tests at the renowned Mayo Clinic in Minnesota. The doctors put him through many tests and concluded that he was suffering from a form of polio called amyotrophic lateral sclerosis. It was called ALS for short, but Americans would soon know it as "Lou Gehrig's disease." All these years later, there is no understanding of what causes it, or how to cure it.

There was some feeling that Lou was never told exactly what he had, but many close to him said he understood the seriousness of his condition. He was losing weight and losing his strength.

The Yankees decided to hold a Lou Gehrig Appreciation Day on July 4, inviting back members of the 1927 Yankees and bringing them on the field with the current Yankees and the visiting team, the Washington Senators. Yankee Stadium was packed for a holiday doubleheader on what would come to be considered the team's first Old-Timers' Day.

Between games, ceremonies were held. Many were weeping, knowing they would never see the Iron Horse play again.

Without any prepared notes, Lou went to the microphone and delivered what some consider baseball's Gettysburg Address—its most famous speech. In it, he talked about the great teammates who had assembled for him that day, talked about his family, and said, "Fans, for the past two weeks you have been reading about a bad break I got. Yet today I consider myself the luckiest man on the face of the earth. . . . So I close in saying that I might have had a bad break, but I have an awful lot to live for. Thank you."

At that point, Babe Ruth, who had not been close to Lou for a long time,

Babe Ruth embracing Lou Gehrig at Lou Gehrig Appreciation Day, July 4, 1939. (Rogers Photo Archives)

stepped forward and put his old teammate in a great bear hug. Photographers clicked away at the emotional picture of these two great Yankees. Newsreel cameramen filmed the speech, and it was seen over and over again in movie theaters. Everyone in America knew the Lou Gehrig story, and if they didn't, Hollywood would make sure they did with the production of *Pride of the Yankees,* in which the great movie star Gary Cooper played Lou. The film won an Academy Award.

Lou stayed with the team throughout the season and remained captain. By 1940 his condition was worsening, and he wasn't around as often. And then on June 2, 1941, came news that Lou had died. He was only thirty-seven years old.

"We will never have another captain," said McCarthy. "The position dies with Lou. No one could ever fill those shoes."

CHAPTER 18

Break Up the Yankees!

By the time the Yankees won the 1939 world championship, it was almost too easy for them. "Break up the Yankees!" fans of other teams would shout, expressing the frustration of seeing them winning all the time. Fans in other cities were resentful as well as disappointed, year after year.

There was an attempt to try to pass rules to slow them down. One rule said that no team could make a trade with the "pennant winner." That lasted a couple of years, then went away.

The rule hardly mattered. The Yankees were the team great players wanted to play with. And in the days when a great prospect could choose his own team, the Yankees had an edge. And so when Tony Lazzeri began to fade at second base, they had Joe Gordon ready to take over. When Frank Crosetti began to fade at shortstop, Phil Rizzuto was ready.

And Joe McCarthy knew how to handle these changes. When Rizzuto arrived in 1941, the older players resented his taking Crosetti's job. It was McCarthy's task to make it happen without bitter feelings. He talked to Crosetti, and he convinced him that change happens, but he would be a real "team player" if he helped it along. And so Crosetti helped Rizzuto learn the position, and Phil, nicknamed "Scooter," and standing just five feet six inches tall, became an All-Star. And Crosetti, when his career ended, became the team's third-base coach. Between his days as a player and as a coach, he wound up being in twenty-three World Series and cashing all those World Series checks.

On September 11, 1940, the Yankees were in third place, but close enough to the top that if they could win a doubleheader that day in Cleveland, they would be in first.

But if it was possible to have one day when nothing went right, the Yankees found it that afternoon. The weather was rainy and miserable, and if it hadn't been a Sunday doubleheader with a big crowd expected, it might have been called off.

It was so gloomy that it was hard to see the outfielders from the dugout. The fans were in a foul mood and began throwing garbage at the Yankees' first- and third-base coaches. McCarthy wanted the umpires to call the game, but they played on.

They beat the fastball sensation Bob Feller in the first game 3–1 despite the miserable conditions, and then sent Ruffing out for game two. With the win in game one, they were actually in first place for the moment.

In the third inning, leading 2–0, Babe Dahlgren dropped a throw at first that led to an Indians rally, and Cleveland took a 5–2 lead. It would probably have been a double play to end the inning. After six innings, the umpires finally stopped the game, and the Indians won, 5–3. They had split the doubleheader, and the Yankees fell out of first.

They never got back. They finished the season in third place, and McCarthy told the sportswriters, "If Dahlgren doesn't drop that throw, we win the game, stay in first, and probably win the pennant."

Of course, he could have been wrong. But if there was one bad day he always looked back on, it was that day—because had the Yankees won the 1940 pennant, history now shows that they would have won eight pennants in a row. And all in Joe DiMaggio's first eight seasons! It was unimaginable.

As for Dahlgren, his Yankee days were numbered, and the little left in his career was undistinguished. He always felt that McCarthy never forgave him for dropping the throw and ran him out of baseball. Could it have been true? Perhaps. There was usually little room for error on the Yankees, and that dropped throw was a big one.

Yankee players were always good at policing one another. If a young player made a mental mistake on the field, he was likely to hear from a veteran after the game, telling him, "Hey, rookie, don't go messing with my World Series money!" And you could be pretty sure that the rookie would not make that mistake again.

Opening day of the following season, 1941, was played in Washington, DC, and as was often the case for opening day in that city, the president was on hand to throw out the first ball. There was President Franklin Roosevelt doing the honors, and there was rookie Phil Rizzuto, the shortstop, taking it all in. He couldn't believe his good fortune.

Rizzuto was a likable fellow with a great sense of humor, and despite his height, he was a star with the Yankees on through 1956. He was such a fan favorite that when his career ended, he became a popular broadcaster for the team until 1996. Many people grew up listening to "Scooter" Rizzuto without even knowing what a star player he was.

Scooter got his nickname from the way he "scooted" after ground balls. Teammates loved to pick on him. He was kind of a quirky guy. He was afraid of bugs. He was afraid of lightning. He rested his chewing gum on top of his cap when he batted.

Joe McCarthy took Scooter under his wing. He sat next to him in the dugout when the Yankees were batting.

"Don't look at the scoreboard," he would say. "Quick—what's the count? How many out?"

He was teaching Rizzuto to use his head, to be more into the game, to pay better attention to the surroundings.

"He was a great man," said Rizzuto. "He knew so much, and he knew how to make each of us better."

During the coming season, McCarthy, Rizzuto—the whole team—were about to witness one of the great feats in baseball history.

On May 15, 1941, DiMaggio got a single in four at bats. He got a hit the next day and the next day and the next. On June 8, he ran his batting streak to twenty-four games, and it was believed that the team record was twenty-nine. (It was actually thirty-three, but that wasn't uncovered until years later. Research was a little sloppy before computers were used for baseball records.)

Joe passed twenty-nine and thirty-three, and now the whole nation started to follow his hitting streak. It was thrilling!

"Did Joe get a hit today?" people asked each other. Even a popular song was recorded, called "Joltin' Joe DiMaggio."

Sportswriters knew that he'd had that sixty-one-game streak in the minors. But this was major league baseball, facing the best of the best every day.

On June 29, Joe passed George Sisler for the "modern" major league record of forty-one. (Modern is used to describe major league baseball after the American League was formed in 1901.) But this was not without adventure! In the second game of a doubleheader in Washington, Joe noticed that his bat was missing. His favorite bat, the one he had been using throughout the streak.

Joe was in a panic. He had to use borrowed bats, and they didn't produce a hit. Finally he borrowed one from Tommy Henrich—and got a hit to pass Sisler. But where was the missing bat?

As it turned out, the bat had been stolen by a fan from New Jersey, and he was doing a lot of bragging about what he'd done. So friends of Joe made things right and got the bat back. No one knew for sure how they got it back or what "offer" they made to the culprit.

What a relief it was for Joe.

At the time, the hitting streak to beat was Wee Willie Keeler's old-time record of forty-four games, set in 1897 (before he joined the Highlanders).

Newspapers and radio reports kept everyone informed. On Joe went—forty-two, forty-three, forty-four, forty-five—a new record! And still, he went on.

There have been few moments in sports as riveting as a popular player going after a record like this, where every day brought suspense.

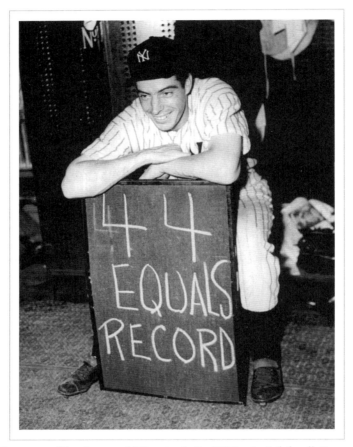

On his way to a fifty-six-game hitting streak, Joe DiMaggio tied the all-time record when he reached forty-four. (Rogers Photo Archive)

In Cleveland, on July 16, Joe ran the streak to fifty-six games in a row. During that time he had batted .408, gotten ninety-one hits, scored fifty-six runs, and driven in fifty-five. He hit fifteen home runs. And now came game fifty-seven, in big Municipal Stadium in Cleveland, where the Indians played on Sundays and holidays only. Big crowd days.

Joe took a cab to the park with Lefty Gomez. "Make sure you get a hit your first time up," said the cabdriver. "If you don't, you'll be stopped!"

Joe was as superstitious as most players and hated hearing that. He believed it was bad luck.

But that day the streak ended. It took two great plays at third base by Kenny Keltner and good pitching by Al Smith and Jim Bagby Jr., but the streak was over at fifty-six.

Joe got a hit in the next game and began a new streak that reached seventeen. So he actually hit safely in seventy-three out of seventy-four games that summer!

Fifty-six remains a hitting streak record more than seventy years later—it's considered one of the greatest achievements in sports history.

Meanwhile, Ted Williams in Boston was making 1941 memorable too. In his third season, he was on his way to batting .406. He is the last player to close out a season above .400, a record that remains seventy plus years later. Between DiMaggio's streak and Williams's batting average, 1941 saw two amazing feats. DiMaggio would win the Most Valuable Player award, but for the rest of their lives, Joe and Ted were spoken of with awe by fans everywhere.

There was a time, some years later, that the owners of the Yankees and the Red Sox briefly considered trading DiMaggio and Williams for each other, since Yankee Stadium would be a better park for the left-hand-hitting Williams, and Fenway Park would be better for the right-hand-hitting DiMaggio. But when the owners woke up the next morning, they called it off. The two meant too much to their existing teams.

The Yankees beat the Brooklyn Dodgers in the 1941 World Series. The key play came in game four, with the Dodgers leading 4–3 in the ninth, and two outs. Brooklyn's Hugh Casey struck out Henrich to end the game, tying the Series at two wins each.

But wait!

Henrich struck out, but Dodger catcher Mickey Owen dropped the ball! It rolled away, and Henrich got to first safely. A passed ball! The Yankees were alive!

DiMaggio singled, Charlie Keller doubled, Bill Dickey walked, and Joe Gordon doubled. Five O'Clock Lightning! The Yankees won it 7–4 and took a three games-to-one lead in the Series that had looked like it was about to be 2–2.

The next day the Yankees won their ninth world championship.

"Taking advantage of an opportunity!" said Yankee fans.

"Dumb Yankee luck," said people who hated the Yankees winning all the time.

But that's baseball.

Tommy Henrich races to first after Brooklyn catcher Mickey Owen's passed ball on strike three in the 1941 World Series. The Yankees rallied to win. (Rogers Photo Archive)

CHAPTER 19

The War Years

The 1941 World Series would mark the end of baseball—and of everyday life in America—as people knew it, at least for the next four years. On December 7, 1941, the Japanese attacked the United States, bombing the US Navy base at Pearl Harbor in Hawaii. Suddenly the nation was at war—both with the Japanese and, soon, with Germany and Italy on the European front. For the next four years, baseball was played by men who were mostly unqualified to be in the service (too old, or suffering from some injury), and a very different level of baseball was played.

There was thought given to suspending baseball until the war was over. Commissioner Landis wrote to President Roosevelt, asking his advice. FDR responded by asking that the game go on, for it would be such a great morale booster for the people back home. People who worked hard hours in factories needed the national pastime as a break in their lives. And so baseball, like the movie industry, continued.

The Yankees, along with other teams, would lose their big stars—notably DiMaggio and Rizzuto—to military service through the draft, but not until

1943. And so in 1942 it was another season, pretty much at full strength—and another championship. They did not win the World Series—the St. Louis Cardinals did—but it marked the seventh time in eight years with DiMaggio that they were in it.

There were travel restrictions imposed during the war to preserve gasoline, and part of that meant the Yankees would be interrupting their ritual of going to St. Petersburg, Florida, for spring training. They had trained there since 1925. Now spring training would be in colder northern climates like Atlantic City and Asbury Park, New Jersey, where the emphasis was on getting in shape more than on playing exhibition games. For the players, "getting in shape" in springtime was critical in those days, long before the current era, when players make big salaries and can afford to not have second jobs in the winter and therefore devote the off-season to staying in shape. Back then, players had no time to work out—they were supporting families by selling insurance, working in warehouses, building roads, or whatever was available to them.

New players arrived during the war, excused from military service for one reason or another. They came from the minor leagues or from other organizations. A slugging first baseman named Nick Etten, a scrappy second baseman named Snuffy Stirnweiss, and a rugged third baseman named Billy Johnson all joined the Yankees during the war.

Catching was still handled by the great Bill Dickey, who at thirty-six was excused from service due to his age. He took advantage of the weaker pitching in the wartime league and batted .351. Eventually, when more and more American soldiers were needed, Dickey too went off to war.

Despite the changes on all the rosters, despite the decreased attendance and everything else being smaller in baseball, the Yankees won again in 1943. It would be the last pennant for manager McCarthy, and right-hander Spud Chandler had a 20–4 record to lead the way and win the Most Valuable Player award. He was the first pitcher in the American League to win it since the Baseball Writers' Association began voting on the award in 1931.

Again the Yankees would face the Cardinals in the World Series. They were looking for revenge from 1942 and found it, winning in five games. The world might have changed, but the Yankees were, for the tenth time, world champions, even while war raged around the world. Chandler hurled a shutout to win the final game 2–0, with Dickey hitting a homer.

The following season, in 1944, there was another new face at Yankee Stadium, and it wasn't the manager or the coaches. It was a high school kid named "Commie" Villante, who presented himself at the ballpark and asked Pop Logan, the clubhouse man, if he could help out. The "help out" resulted in his being hired as the batboy.

For young Yankee fans, being a batboy always seemed like a dream job. You got to know the players, you got to wear the uniform, you got to shag fly balls during batting practice, you got into the team photo, and all your friends thought you were the coolest guy around. Everyone wanted to be "that guy."

But it was also a hard job, carrying heavy equipment bags, running errands for the players, being alert during the games for foul balls onto the screen—and all for just a few bucks a game, plus an occasional tip from a player.

Fans always remembered batboy Eddie Bennett from the Babe Ruth years. Bennett was not actually a boy at all, but a handicapped adult with a deformed back. Babe's mascot, Little Ray, was too young to carry bat bags, and was never a batboy—just a good luck mascot.

Logan, who had been with the team since its beginning, liked that Commie was athletic and wouldn't step all over himself on the field. Villante worked hard at the job, managing to be a batboy as well as continue his high school education. He was coached by Crosetti, and sometimes he even got to stand side by side with Stirnweiss at second during infield practice.

McCarthy noticed Villante's hard work and playing ability and, on behalf of the Yankees, offered Commie a four-year scholarship to the college of his choice. He chose Lafayette, where he played varsity second base for four years. McCarthy thought he might graduate and perhaps play second for the Yanks.

But after graduation, there were no open positions, and McCarthy was no longer there, so Villante joined a big New York advertising agency and changed his name to Tommy Villante.

Tommy "Commie" Villante was a Yankees batboy who later became the director of broadcasting and marketing for major league baseball. (Tom Villante)

Villante's advertising firm represented the beer sponsor of the Dodgers games, and when television came along, he became the producer of the games. He even went from Brooklyn to Los Angeles when the Dodgers moved west in 1958, and continued to produce the games there.

Later he joined major league baseball as director of broadcasting and marketing and created the slogan, "Baseball Fever: Catch It." He maintained hundreds of friendships in the game and was an example of someone who really took advantage of his opportunity as batboy—working hard, being respectful, not complaining about the low pay, showing a great personality, and being smart and honest. He never swiped a baseball, never bothered players for autographs when they were busy, and always listened to his bosses.

The batboy jobs remain jobs that many kids want, and after Commie, first Harry Jacobs and then Joe Carrieri became the lead batboys from 1946 to 1955. And since the players usually voted a slice of World Series money to the batboys, Harry and Joe picked up seven bonus checks between them.

Alas, in 1944 and 1945, there would be no World Series checks for Villante. But he couldn't complain about a four-year college scholarship and had the experience of a lifetime.

At last, in 1945, the war was over. The players would be coming home, and so would the fans. America was filled with pride over winning the war, and the national pastime at its best was part of what so many had missed.

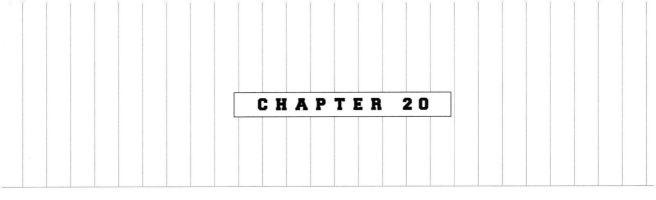

CHAPTER 20

Yogi

The Yankees now had new owners. For six years Ed Barrow had run the club while three women named by Ruppert in his will had owned the team. In 1945 they finally sold it to a land developer named Del Webb, a sportsman/businessman named Dan Topping, and a baseball executive named Larry MacPhail, who had run the Cincinnati Reds and the Brooklyn Dodgers.

MacPhail was the one who was most in charge. He was a very promotion-minded baseball man. He made major changes to Yankee Stadium, installing lights for night games (starting in 1946) and adding restaurants, a press dining room, and new box seats to the stadium. He redesigned the team's clubhouses, moved the offices to a swanky Fifth Avenue address, and created Old-Timer's Day, an event to salute former players, as an annual tradition. He hired a public relations director and got the team to occasionally fly to road games. He hired an artist to design a new logo for the team, and the artist came up with the idea of a patriotic "Uncle Sam" top hat on top of the letter *K* in Yankees (the *K* being partly a baseball bat), with the word surrounded by a baseball. It became one of the best-known logos in sports.

MacPhail's flamboyant style was never going to work with McCarthy, who was resistant to change, particularly when MacPhail involved himself in roster moves or criticized players. In 1945 one of the Yankees' best pitchers, Hank Borowy, was 10–5 in midseason, and MacPhail sold him to the Chicago Cubs. It happened while McCarthy was on a leave of absence from the Yankees, resting at his home near Buffalo, New York. He couldn't believe that MacPhail would do such a thing—the Yankees were a very successful team and didn't have to sell good players to raise money. But that was what MacPhail was used to doing with his previous teams.

It didn't help McCarthy's mood any when Borowy went 11–2 with the Cubs and helped them win the pennant.

As for who would outlast who, McCarthy or MacPhail, the writers who covered the team were betting on MacPhail. After all, he was part-owner, and if you were going to clash with an owner, your chances were not very good.

And in 1946, McCarthy's days with the team came to an end. Even though the Yankees were leading the major league postwar revival, with more than 2,250,000 fans attending Yankee home games, and DiMaggio, Rizzuto, and all the rest were back, McCarthy was miserable. Not only did he not get along with MacPhail, but his health was not good, and on May 24 he announced his resignation. Some called it a retirement, but they were wrong—he would return to manage the Red Sox in 1948. In the meantime, he was leaving with eight pennants, seven world championships, and the admiration of his players and the fans.

Bill Dickey would take over as manager, but when he couldn't get a promise of a contract extension into 1947, he resigned, leaving Johnny Neun, a coach, to finish out the year of chaos and confusion as manager. It was not a pennant season, to say the least.

The mess that was 1946 needed to be straightened out for '47, and so the Yankees turned to an old-time baseball figure, Bucky Harris, to manage the team. Bucky was fifty and had already managed for twenty years in the big leagues, beginning with the Washington Senators in 1924. In fact, in that very first season, at age twenty-seven, he was a player-manager and had led his team to the world championship. He won the pennant again in 1925 but hadn't been back to the Series since. Now he had the Yankees job.

The year 1947 has come to be known to historians as a milestone year. It was the year the Brooklyn Dodgers brought Jackie Robinson to the major leagues, ending the unwritten ban on black ballplayers. While it took baseball a long time to see this day, it also preceded the nation's attention to civil rights and laws to protect minorities by at least seven years. Baseball was, in fact, leading the way.

The Yankees, however, were not fast to sign black players. In 1949 they signed two for the minor leagues, but it wasn't until 1955 that one made the major league team.

Bucky Harris had a catcher on the '47 team named Lawrence Peter "Yogi" Berra. When he was a kid in St. Louis, a teammate had called him "Yogi" because he was sitting outside his dugout with his legs folded as though in a yoga position. Talk about a nickname that stuck—it wouldn't be long before everyone in America knew Yogi.

His nickname helped to make him popular, but he had a great backstory, too. He had quit school in the eighth grade to help out his family during the Depression. He continued to play sandlot ball with his pal Joe Garagiola, as they both developed their skills. Joe eventually signed with the Cardinals, and Yogi with the Yankees. Two kids from the same block!

Yogi did not look like a player—he was short and a little round. The first day he showed up in the Yankees clubhouse, he was still wearing his navy uniform. (He had served in World War II—the only major league player at D-Day in Normandy.) The clubhouse manager, Pete Sheehy, paid little attention to him, not realizing he was a ballplayer. "I guess he didn't look like a player?" someone asked.

"He didn't even look like a sailor," responded Pete.

He wasn't a great interview subject because he tended to grunt a lot and give short answers. But the sportswriters began to realize that although his answers tended to sound funny, they often made a lot of sense.

Yogi Berra joined the Yankees in 1946 after his navy discharge. He had fought at D-Day in Normandy during World War II. (Rogers Photo Archives)

Some years later, Yogi's boyhood pal from St. Louis, Joe Garagiola, became a well-known broadcaster and speaker, and he used to tell Yogi stories, some real, and some made up.

"Hey, Yogi, how do we get to your house?"

And Yogi might say, "When you come to a fork in the road—take it."

"Hey Yogi, how did you manage to switch from outfielder to catcher so well?"

And Yogi answered, "Bill Dickey—he learned me all of his experience."

"Hey, Yogi, can we go back to that restaurant we went to last time?"

"Nobody goes there anymore," he answered. "It's too crowded."

Another great anecdote about Yogi is that during his early days playing with the Yankees, he roomed with third baseman Bobby Brown. Brown was studying to become a doctor and would read his medical books at night, while Yogi preferred comic books. One night it was time to shut out the lights, and Yogi said to Bobby, "How did your book turn out?"

Yogi's jokes may have made him seem a little dumb, but he was anything but. When it came to his profession, he was a genius. Yogi had a great batting eye and seldom struck out. He could foul off a lot of pitches until he got the one he wanted. And he became a great handler of pitchers, too, memorizing each batter's weaknesses. It wasn't long before he was practically an assistant manager on the field. He would go on to win three Most Valuable Player awards. He would play in fourteen World Series and set many lifetime batting records for Series play. He was an All-Star every year from 1948 to 1962. Fifteen straight years an All-Star!

In Yogi's first season, 1947, the Yankees were a team in transition. It was also the first season their games were shown on television for all to see. (Or at least "all" who owned television sets—which were not yet that many people.) Besides their new manager and Berra, the Yankees had a new relief star in Joe Page, and a new starting pitcher named Allie Reynolds. They traded second baseman Joe Gordon to the Cleveland Indians for Reynolds, who turned out to be one of the best starting pitchers they ever had. A Native American from Oklahoma, Allie was all business on the mound, and as his career progressed, he showed he was also able to pitch in relief between starts, with great success.

Reynolds would be joined in the starting rotation by Vic Raschi, "the Springfield Rifle" (for the town he came from in Massachusetts), and Eddie Lopat, a left-hander who did not throw very hard. "Junkballs," they called them. But those "junkballs" were very effective. For years, Reynolds, Raschi, and Lopat formed the best three-man rotation the team ever had. For fans buying tickets, it didn't really matter which of the three was on the mound that day—the Yankees always had a good chance to win with any of them out there.

Even though the Yankees were in need of straightening out when he joined them, Bucky Harris had taken on a really fine ball club, and when the Yankees won nineteen games in a row during the summer, they were clearly on their

"Steady Eddie" Lopat was a slow-balling "junk pitcher" who had great success with the Yankees.
(Rogers Photo Archives)

way to a pennant. The year before, Harris had been stuck with Buffalo in the minor leagues. And now this. The mighty New York Yankees, heading to a World Series. What an opportunity!

The 1947 World Series was the first one to be televised, and it was a dandy. It was the Yankees against the Brooklyn Dodgers, with Jackie Robinson in his historic first season.

Yogi hit the first pinch-hit home run in World Series history. It was a long time coming.

But game four was the one everyone would talk about. There had never been a no-hitter in a World Series game, and now the Yankees pitcher Bill Bevens had one through eight innings. What a ninth inning this would be.

Some fans, and even some players, didn't realize there was a no-hitter in progress, because Bevens was wild. He had walked eleven batters, and it seemed like men were always in scoring position, but there it was on the scoreboard—no hits, and a 2–1 Yankee lead. It was hardly a masterpiece, but it was still a no-hitter.

So in the ninth, with excitement brewing, Bevens found two pinch runners on base—Al Gionfriddo and Eddie Miksis, with pinch hitter Cookie Lavagetto coming to bat. "Lookie, lookie, here comes Cookie," the Dodgers fans liked to say.

The count was 1-and-1 on Cookie, and the next pitch was high and away. Lavagetto swung and drove it over right fielder Tommy Henrich's glove for the first hit of the game. Gionfriddo and Miksis both scored, as announcer Red Barber told his radio audience, "Here comes the tying run and here comes the WINNING run!" With one pitch, the no-hitter and the victory were gone. It was a devastating game ending for the Yankees.

There was another big moment in game six, when Gionfriddo raced back to rob DiMaggio of what looked like a home run. Joe had eight World Series home runs in his career but had never hit one in Yankee Stadium. This looked like it was the one, but as Red Barber announced, "Gionfriddo . . . back, back, back, back, back, back . . . he makes a one-handed catch against the bull pen! Oh doctor!" (Today you can hear ESPN's Chris Berman do a Red Barber imitation when he calls the Home Run Derby at the All-Star Game each year.)

DiMaggio, sure that he had a big homer, kicked the dirt as he headed for second and realized it was just a long out. It was about the only time anyone had seen Joe show emotion on the field.

The Yankees did win game seven though, and again, they were world champions. It was a great World Series, but right after the game, Larry MacPhail, who had been drinking all afternoon, went into the clubhouse celebration and told the press, "That's it for me! I'm selling my interest in the team and retiring from baseball!"

This was considered really bad form, taking the spotlight away from the players after they had won the World Series.

That very night, everyone associated with the Yankees headed down to the Biltmore Hotel near Grand Central Terminal for a celebration party.

The party didn't go well for Larry MacPhail. He was angry with everyone, and he got into an argument with the respected George Weiss, the man who had succeeded Ed Barrow as general manager after having been the longtime minor-league director.

Clubhouse celebration scenes were frequent with the Yankees. Here are (left to right) Vic Raschi, Yogi Berra, and Bill Bevens. (Rogers Photo Archives)

And before anyone knew what had happened, MacPhail punched Weiss and fired him!

"Take that!" he said. "And you're fired, too!"

Weiss hadn't said anything. He almost never said anything to anybody. But he got punched out right there at the World Series party! It came to be called the "Battle of the Biltmore." The sportswriters all saw it, and it was an embarrassing moment for the organization, and the second embarrassing incident for MacPhail that very day.

MacPhail managed to get more publicity that day than the Yankees did in winning the World Series. Larry MacPhail's nickname, the "Roaring Redhead," had proven apt on that last day on which he owned part of the Yankees.

The next day Dan Topping and Del Webb bought out MacPhail's one-third ownership of the team, and MacPhail left baseball forever. His baseball legacy lived on in his well-mannered son Lee, who would one day be the Yankees general manager, and in his grandson Andy, who would one day be general manager of the Twins and president of the Cubs and the Orioles.

But with MacPhail gone, ol' Bucky Harris was in a tough spot in 1948. Bucky would probably not survive a season in which the Yankees didn't win it all. George Weiss was restored as general manager the day MacPhail left and was anxious to put his own stamp on the team without MacPhail's interference.

But the Yankees did not have a pennant in them. They won ninety-four games and finished third, just two and a half games out of first. Harris was fired.

Imagine how history can turn on such things. Surely there were a few games during 1948 that got away, that might have been wins. Joe Page had a bad year and blew some saves. Ninety-four wins was pretty good.

If Harris had won three more games, and the Yankees had won the pennant, he would probably not have been fired. What was to come—fourteen pennants in the next sixteen years—might all have been his. He might have won sixteen pennants in eighteen years, and might have kept going from there.

Regardless of his unceremonious ousting, Bucky Harris made the Hall of Fame in 1975, based on his twenty-nine seasons of managing and those "Boy Wonder" pennants in the 1920s. If he'd won sixteen pennants in eighteen years, he might have been considered the greatest manager who ever lived, and certainly an immortal name in Yankees history.

But he just couldn't find those three extra wins in 1948. Who knows what might have been?

There were two famous farewells for Babe Ruth at Yankee Stadium near the end of his life. Dying of cancer, he was honored in both 1947 and 1948, his uniform number 3 retired, and most people in attendance were saddened by the fact that Babe looked very ill. When he died at age fifty-three in 1948, thousands of fans came to Yankee Stadium one last time to view his body before the funeral.

There was never anyone like Babe Ruth. And oh, what he meant to the Yankees!

CHAPTER 21

Casey

George Weiss chose a very surprising, and unlikely, new manager for the Yankees.

He picked Casey Stengel, whose career went back to 1910, and who came from Kansas City, Missouri—which is how he got his nickname of K.C.—or "Casey."

Stengel was the man who lost his shoe—or thought he did—running the bases on an inside-the-park home run at Yankee Stadium in 1923. He had always been seen as somewhat of a clownish figure in baseball. He once tipped his cap and a bird flew out.

Before he pursued baseball, Stengel had originally hoped to become a dentist. But back then it was almost impossible to be a left-handed dentist. The equipment was made for right-handers.

He had played for a lot of teams and managed a lot of teams, all in the National League and the minor leagues. In the National League, he had managed for nine years without ever finishing higher than fifth. He would be taking over a veteran team with players who hustled for Joe McCarthy and thought McCarthy was the model manager. Weiss knew Casey from an early minor-league managing job in the twenties. Everyone in baseball knew Casey, who could be the life of any party.

The sportswriters liked the selection of Casey. He was a fun guy—fun to be around. He enjoyed telling stories late into the night, keeping the hotel bar open until all hours, and entertaining people with tales about the days he played for John McGraw, or the years he was part of the Daffiness Boys of Brooklyn, a team so nicknamed because they had a number of zany players like Casey.

Not many people took Casey Stengel seriously when the Yankees named him manager in 1949, but he proved them wrong. (Rogers Photo Archives)

He looked, well, funny. He seemed older than his years, and the writers took to calling him "the Ol' Professor." He talked funny—Stengelese, they called it. It was his way of avoiding answers. He would double-talk. Tommy Henrich was "Handricks." And writers would laugh. The players always seemed to know what he was saying.

Photographers and cartoonists loved him because his wrinkled face lent itself to terrific portraits.

His reputation as a manager was not especially good. When managing the

Boston Braves in the early 1940s, he was run over by a cabdriver and forced to stay home for a long stretch. A Boston sportswriter suggested giving the cabdriver an award as the person "who did the most for Boston baseball this year."

Although he had a year to go on his Braves contract, he was fired after the 1943 season and "paid not to manage" in 1944. He had been in the minor leagues ever since, but had success with the Oakland Oaks of the Pacific Coast League, winning the pennant.

He had never had the luxury of talented players before, but he would learn to make the most of the Yankees' talent, and his system became "two-platoon baseball." Today we see it a lot—right-handed hitters against left-handed pitchers, lefties against righties. (Pitchers usually have an advantage if the batter hits from the same side as they throw.) Back then, it was a novel idea because there weren't a lot of statistics to work with. And so where he could, he played people on hunches or memory of certain success against certain matchups. If he had five really good outfielders, he would move them in and out of the lineup, and he usually seemed to get it right. Not all the players liked this, even if it was helping the team to win.

Only Yogi played every day during this era, and in his final years, so would DiMaggio. But DiMaggio, and others who had played for McCarthy, didn't really like Stengel. They missed McCarthy.

Players had to check the lineup when they got to the ballpark and take nothing for granted. Even starting pitchers would look for a baseball in their shoe when they got to the park, a signal from pitching coach Jim Turner that they were working that day.

When he joined the Yankees, Casey Stengel brought a second baseman named Billy Martin with him from his Oakland team. Billy was unlike any other Yankee player. His talents were questionable. He was never going to be a superstar on his own limited abilities. But he wore his Yankees uniform with such pride that it was like a superhero costume with a cape, giving him superpowers that exceeded his abilities. Few Yankees in history ever got so much out of their abilities as he did. Skinny as a rail, he hit only .262 for the Yankees over seven seasons, and in only three of them did he play more than a hundred games. But his star really shone in World Series games, where he set batting records, made historic catches, and won Most Valuable Player awards. Casey loved him, and he came to be known as "Casey's Boy." He was such a smart player that he saw things others did not. Eventually he would be known as a brilliant manager—including time spent managing the Yankees.

But discipline was not well suited to Martin. He was a rule breaker, like the Babe. He drank too much, and it often got him into fights. He came to see himself as an old-time Western cowboy gunslinger, looking for a challenge. Over his career he was in about a dozen fights—with players, team officials, sportswriters, fans—enough to cause him to get traded or fired a lot. But as a player, he would know a lot of glory days.

In 1949, Casey's first year managing, the Yankees had seventy-one injuries, and he had to move players in and out, try them in new positions, and juggle his lineup almost every day. Only fifteen times did DiMaggio, Berra, and Henrich appear together in the lineup. If "two-platoon baseball" hadn't been his style, this season would have forced him to invent it.

He had Hank Bauer and Gene Woodling, two fine outfielders, taking turns against lefty or righty pitching. He learned to use Jerry Coleman, an infielder, at second, short, or third. Another infielder who would come along two years later, Gil McDougald, also played all three positions, depending on the needs of the day. This was Casey at his best. And McDougald was an All-Star selection at all three.

Among the injured was DiMaggio, who had a heel injury. He didn't play until June 28. Suddenly waking up and feeling good, Joe took a plane to Boston and told Casey he was ready to go.

In what would become a memorable series in Joe's career and Yankee history, DiMaggio proceeded to homer that very night, then hit two more the next day and another one in the final game—four home runs in four games! So excited was everyone by this great return that the Yankees held a Joe DiMaggio Day on October 1, with almost seventy thousand coming to Yankee Stadium to honor him.

In his speech, Joe said, "I'd like to thank the good Lord for making me a Yankee."

Years later that sentence was painted on the wall leading from the Yankee clubhouse to the dugout, and each day, Derek Jeter would touch it for good luck.

The '49 Yankees won the pennant and returned to the World Series, again playing the Brooklyn Dodgers.

Casey's very first World Series game as a manager was a great pitching duel between Reynolds and the Dodgers's Don Newcombe. In the last of the ninth of a 0–0 tie, Henrich led off with a walk-off home run to deep right field. What a game! What a moment!

The Dodgers won the second game 1–0, but that was all they could muster, as the Yanks won in five, with DiMaggio homering in the deciding game.

It was a great triumph for Stengel, who had never had managing success before. Suddenly he was looking like a genius in his first season.

Allie Reynolds, a Native American, shown here with Joe DiMaggio, starred as both a starter and a reliever for the Yanks. (Rogers Photo Archives)

CHAPTER 22

Whitey and Mickey

On July 1, 1950, Whitey Ford made his major league debut.

Ed "Whitey" Ford was only five foot ten and didn't throw hard, but he learned a lot about pitching from Lefty Gomez, who had been his minor league manager, and Eddie Lopat, now his Yankee teammate. He was a left-hander who would go on to win more games than any Yankee pitcher in history, and more World Series games than anyone in history—ten. Whitey was a local player, raised in Queens (with a perfect attendance record in school), and he had New York "smarts." He played first base as a kid because he was thought to be too small to pitch. That sounds like nonsense, but he is actually the only pitcher from the second half of the twentieth century under six feet tall to get to the Hall of Fame.

Nothing about being in the big New York spotlight seemed to bother Ford, even at age twenty. He would come to gain another nickname besides Whitey, and that was "Slick." When he was winning sixteen games at Binghamton in his third year in the minor leagues, he stopped at a pay phone one day and called the Yankee offices to ask why he wasn't being brought up to the majors. He hadn't even pitched in Triple-A yet!

Whitey joined Reynolds, Raschi, and Lopat in the Yankees pitching rotation and proceeded to win his first nine decisions in the major leagues. His only loss that year came in a relief appearance in the final days of the season. He was already a sensation.

Late in the season, the Yankees picked up longtime National League slugger Johnny Mize. Many felt Mize was nearing the end of a great career, but he proceeded to belt twenty-five home runs and drove in seventy-two runs with only seventy-six hits. This began a new phase in Yankee success: picking up old veterans in midseason and finding a way to get terrific outputs from them. The practice was still going in 2013 when they got Alfonso Soriano from the Cubs, and he produced big-time, just as Mize had done.

The Yankees won the 1950 pennant and faced the Philadelphia Phillies in the World Series. It was the first pennant for the Phillies since 1915, but they didn't have much time to celebrate, as the Yankees quickly won the first three games and sent Ford to the mound for game four.

The rookie had no trouble with the "Whiz Kids," as the Phillies were called. In the ninth, with the Yankees leading 5–2 and two out, Stengel went to the mound and motioned for Allie Reynolds to come in for the final out.

Instead of cheering Ford, as would be expected, the Yankee Stadium crowd booed Stengel for removing the new young hero. But Reynolds got the last out, and it was two world championships in a row for Casey.

Ford wasn't the only great new player to join the Yankees in that era. One particular scout had found the team's next big star.

Before computers began to log high school and college players in America, scouting was almost like working for the CIA. It was very secretive, and it was possible for a good scout to find a player that no one had heard of.

That was the case for scout Tom Greenwade. He had gotten a tip about a seventeen-year-old named Mickey Mantle, who played in the northeast corner of Oklahoma, just a few miles from Missouri, Kansas, and Arkansas in any direction. It was at a game in Baxter Springs, Kansas, in 1948 where Tom first saw the heavily muscled Mantle sock long home runs from both sides of the plate.

What a great name "Mickey Mantle" was. Mickey was not a nickname—his dad had named him after his own favorite player, Gordon "Mickey" Cochrane, an old-time catcher. But it really sounded like a name made up in Hollywood.

Mick was still a junior in high school, so he wasn't eligible to sign for another year, until his senior class graduated. Greenwade kept an eye on him. He was not a very good shortstop, but a move to the outfield would solve that. He had tremendous speed and power. He learned to switch-hit when his father (Mutt) and his grandfather (Charles) threw righty and lefty to him against a tin storage shed next to the Mantle home. Mutt was a miner in Commerce, Oklahoma, and that could easily have been Mickey's future too, going into the zinc mines and doing hard labor every day. But the boy could play baseball.

"The first time I saw Mantle," said Greenwade, "I knew how Paul Krichell felt when he first saw Lou Gehrig."

Mickey missed his graduation ceremony from Commerce High School because he had a game to play in Coffeyville, Kansas. After the game, Greenwade offered Mick a Yankee contract with a bonus of $1,100. Mutt Mantle had to sign it, since Mick was still a minor, but this meant if he played well in the Yankee farm system, he might be a big-league ballplayer.

By 1951, he was considered ready for the major leagues, even though he was still only nineteen years old. He had recovered from a high school football injury and showed terrific speed, especially busting out of the left-hand batter's box and racing to first. He played right field that year, with DiMaggio in center. He still had traces of teenage acne on his face, but his good looks and huge arms got a lot of attention.

"We had heard all about him during spring training," recalled Yogi Berra's wife, Carmen. "On opening day we stayed in the same hotel near Yankee

Stadium. A bunch of wives were in the lobby when the elevator opened and out he came. And we all thought, 'Oh my God, is he handsome!'"

Casey loved teaching him about outfield play, although sometimes Mick would look at him in amazement, as though to say, *You were a player?* Casey must have looked ninety years old to Mantle, all wrinkled as he was.

Maybe he was still a little too young. He hadn't played a season of Triple-A minor league baseball. Pete Sheehy, the clubhouse manager, gave him uniform number 6. The message was clear. Ruth was 3, Gehrig was 4, DiMaggio was 5. Mick was going to be "next in line" as a Yankee great.

But it didn't start off as smoothly as everyone had hoped. Despite hitting a 452-foot home run on May 1, he was struggling with his confidence and with big-league pitching. He was a nineteen-year-old kid from Oklahoma playing next to DiMaggio (who rarely spoke to him). It was the style of the day that the veterans didn't socialize much with the rookies. Their attitude was, "He might be taking the job of a friend of mine!" Mickey never forgot how veterans treated rookies and always tried to welcome new players onto the team and take them to dinner. He later said the best compliment that he ever got was to be called "a great teammate." It's on his plaque in Monument Park. And DiMaggio more or less ignoring Mantle was enough to shake anyone's confidence.

The Yankees decided Mantle did need more seasoning, and they sent him to their top farm team in Kansas City. There he played forty games and batted .361. When he returned, he got number 7 instead of 6. The previous number 7, Bob Cerv, was sent down, and the old number 6, Bobby Brown, had come back from military service and reclaimed his number.

There was another new face on the Yankees in 1951, but this one was in the press box. It was a gentlemanly professor named Bob Sheppard, who taught speech at St. John's University. He was hired to be the public address announcer at Yankee Stadium. His voice, so distinguished and perfect, became a fixture at the stadium for more than fifty years. Visiting players would say, "Bob Sheppard announced my name; now I felt like I was in the major leagues!"

Reggie Jackson would later say, "He sounded like the Voice of God!" And Derek Jeter requested that the recorded voice of Sheppard introducing him be played even after Sheppard died in 2010. The recording was used for the rest of Jeter's career.

CHAPTER 23

The DiMaggio Era Ends

In 1951 Mantle became friends with Billy Martin, and when Whitey Ford returned from military duty two years later, the three of them formed a lifelong friendship. They were young, they were Yankees, they were enjoying success, and they enjoyed the night life that the big cities of major league baseball offered. They were the "three musketeers," and they could drive Casey Stengel crazy by breaking curfew and skirting his rules. But Casey had been a bit of a carouser during his playing days, and he understood. So long as they were playing well, he let them have their fun.

DiMaggio was struggling in 1951. He was bothered again by a painful heel injury, and he was batting well under .300. This was not the Joe DiMaggio that he liked fans to see.

But his best wasn't there anymore. The heel was doing him in.

The Yankees won the '51 pennant and faced the New York Giants in the World Series. The first two games were in Yankee Stadium, with DiMaggio in center and Mantle in right. In the fifth inning of game two, the Giants' great rookie Willie Mays hit a fly ball between them. Mantle raced over to his right,

DiMaggio moved gracefully to his left. When either man can make the play, it is the center fielder who generally calls for it. And DiMaggio did indeed say, at the last moment, "I've got it."

Mantle later said, "It was the first time he talked to me all year!"

Mick pulled up short so that DiMag could make the play, and in so doing, his spikes got caught against a drainage pipe buried in the grass. It was a fluke accident. Mantle collapsed and was carried off on a stretcher. He had torn his ACL—a ligament in his knee.

Three great buddies, three championship players—(left to right) Whitey Ford, Mickey Mantle, and Billy Martin. (Ozzie Sweet photo; courtesy of Randall Swearingen)

Still the Yanks won 3–1. But Mantle missed the rest of the Series and wound up sharing a hospital room with his dad, who was dying of cancer. Mutt Mantle got to see only the one year of Mick's career—the only year, at age nineteen, in which he played healthy all season. The torn ACL was not operated on for another two years, and Mick would spend the rest of his career wrapping his legs in elastic bandages each day, and suffering other related and unrelated injures along the way. His accomplishments—great as they were—needed to be measured against the serious injuries that always seemed to find him.

Many people thought that without the injuries, he might have been the greatest player in history. He had it all, including speed. Baseball had never seen a switch-hitter with so much power, and the fact that he could beat out bunts for hits—and could run like the wind to catch long fly balls—made him stand out among all the great players who came before him.

The Yankees won their third straight World Series in 1951, and on December 11, DiMaggio announced that "I've played my last game of ball." The year 1951 would be the only year in which Mantle and DiMaggio were teammates.

DiMaggio never left the public stage. He was adored by his generation of fans, and that meant the world to him. Over the remaining forty-eight years of his life, he attended forty-seven Old-Timers' Days. He missed only one year when he was in the hospital. It was important that he hear the roar of the crowd. In 1969 he was voted the Greatest Living Player in a national fan vote, and he always liked to be introduced that way. It meant a lot to him.

After his career, he was briefly married to the greatest movie star of the time, Marilyn Monroe, and they remained close until her death in 1962. He was a constant presence on television commercials for a coffee machine and for a bank. He would always be "the Yankee Clipper" in the hearts and minds of America.

Mantle now had a whole new generation of fans watching his every move. The baby boomers—those born after World War II—adopted him as their favorite. He had it all: the looks, the power, the speed, the boyish smile, and the style. He never showed up an opponent; he always respected the way the game should be played. He wore his uniform "just right."

Because he came along in the 1950s, he soon became baseball's first television star. With more and more homes purchasing TVs, and with the Yankees in the

World Series almost every year, there he was each October on national television, on NBC, the star of the mighty Yankees. There also began a national telecast during the season—the Game of the Week, often involving the Yankees. It was "blacked out" in major league cities, so New York fans knew little about it—but much of the nation got to see the Yankees more than any other team, and there was Mantle, batting third, looking oh so good as he slugged long home runs and ran the bases with his head down, elbows up, and just a little trace of a limp.

He was on the cover of all the magazines—not just sports magazines, but even *Life* and *Time* and *Newsweek* and *TV Guide*.

Baseball cards became popular in the early 1950s when Topps got into the business. While a Mantle "rookie card" from 1952 would become one of the

Mickey Mantle's "rookie card," from 1952, came to be a great collector's item. (The Topps Company)

most sought-after by collectors in later years—worth thousands of dollars—they had no value at the time they were issued, other than kids really wanting them. Sure, some kids put them in their bicycle spokes to make a sound like a motor, and some kids may have traded them for an unknown player they were missing, and some mothers may have thrown them out during a spring cleaning, but everyone seemed to know that the Mantle cards were the ones to get.

One thing that made them extra valuable in later years was that Topps dumped many unsold sheets of cards—including Mantle—into the Upper New York Bay just feet from its Brooklyn office, during a cleanup around 1960. So the Mantles came to be thought of as scarce.

Baseball cards remained an important part of being a young fan. Long before close-ups on TV and color photography in magazines, the cards were the way to get to know the players well. Kids memorized the statistics on the backs and learned about the players' hobbies (mostly hunting and fishing). And as long as he played, Mantle remained the most important card for young fans to collect, not even realizing that one day the cards would be worth thousands of dollars.

CHAPTER 24

The Fiftieth Anniversary

The year 1952 was the Yankees' fiftieth season, and the *New York Times* picked an "all-time Yankee team" to mark the occasion. Babe Ruth, Joe DiMaggio, and Bob Meusel were the outfielders. Gehrig was at first, Lazzeri at second, Rizzuto at short, and Red Rolfe at third. (Rolfe manned the position from 1934–1942 and was a four-time all-star.) Dickey was the catcher, with Gomez and Ruffing the starters (left and right). The Yankees asked their regular sportswriters to pick a team too, and they chose the same players, but added Johnny Murphy as a relief pitcher, Frank Crosetti as a utility man, and Herb Pennock tied with Gomez as the left-handed starter.

By now the Yankees were the most successful team in any professional league. The expectations were always to win the World Series, and now they were on a roll. In '52 they would go for a fourth in a row—just as the Yankees of 1936–1939 had done.

And they did it! They won another pennant, and then another World Series. In the final game, Billy Martin made an amazing catch, running hard toward home plate from second base to catch a short pop at his shoelaces, while Mantle, still just twenty years old, broke a tie with a homer.

The telecast was saved with a process called "kinescope," which was basically a movie camera taking film of the picture on the TV screen. It is the oldest full game in existence that was saved. And while the World Series was always televised, that was not the case with regular season games.

"Is today's game on TV?" one might ask a friend. In New York, fans were lucky and saw as many as 125 games a year on television. Not every city was as fortunate. Today, of course, every game is televised either on cable or broadcast TV, and can also be seen on computer or handheld device—and all over the world, at that. But it was once an occasional occurrence, even in the age of television.

The highlight of the 1953 regular season came on April 17 in Washington, when Mantle hit what may be the longest home run ever recorded. Batting right-handed, he belted one clear out of Griffith Stadium to the amazement of all who saw it.

Red Patterson was the Yankees' public relations director. He left the press box and went out to "measure it." When he returned, he said he had paced it off with his shoes and reported that the ball had traveled 565 feet.

Even though he used his shoes (and there was later some doubt about him leaving the ballpark at all), the blast came to be called a "tape-measure home run." That was the start of measuring homers. The outfield distances were always painted on the fences, but the idea of regularly measuring them started that day. From that point on, Mantle was always the one to watch if long-distance pokes were what you wanted to see. And while no one ever hit a fair ball out of Yankee Stadium, Mickey twice hit the "facade" (or frieze), the portion that hung down from the roof and circled the stadium. His long home runs became legendary.

Helped by an eighteen-game winning streak, the Yankees' twentieth pennant came in 1953, and then they won their fifth straight world championship, with another victory over Brooklyn in the World Series, as Billy Martin delivered twelve hits and batted .500.

Five straight World Series wins!

A dozen players—half the team!—had been there for all of them, and it is possible that five straight will never happen again. After all, in those days a team had to win the pennant (beating seven opponents) and then one round of "play-offs"—the World Series. Today, to win a pennant, a team has to beat fourteen other teams in the league, then win two rounds of play-offs before even getting to the World Series. And of course, it is difficult to keep a star roster together for so long, as free agent opportunities come up.

It is far more difficult to accomplish today, let alone doing it five times in a row. Still, this unprecedented World Series winning streak gave cause for celebration by Yankees fans everywhere.

The streak came to a close in 1954, the year in which a novel was published called *The Year the Yankees Lost the Pennant*. (The book would become a movie and a Broadway show called *Damn Yankees*.) It wasn't that the Yankees did anything wrong. In fact, they won 103 games, the most ever under Stengel. But good as that was, it was eight wins fewer than Cleveland, who set an American League record with 111 victories.

Still, Yankees fans were so accustomed to seeing their team win that the season was a huge disappointment for them. To help make up for it, the team held a fan appreciation day in late September and even handed out a program apologizing for not winning!

CHAPTER 25

Elston Howard Integrates the Yankees

With Jackie Robinson having been in the majors for eight years, and with African-American players on the rosters of both the Dodgers and Giants, it became a source of irritation for many that the Yankees were still an all-white team. Black baseball fans supported the Yankees and went to Yankee Stadium both for their games and for Negro League games when the Yankees leased their park to those teams. Civil rights leaders, whether baseball fans or not, were critical of the Yankees' slowness to integrate.

The Negro Leagues had begun in 1920 and lasted until 1951. It was a place for African-American players to compete while they were banned from the major (and minor) leagues. They were a little disorganized when it came to record keeping, and players jumped from team to team each year quite freely, but they were fun and, of course, had terrific talent—the players who were obviously qualified to play in the majors but were denied the right.

But because the Yankees were winning every year, and leading the league in attendance, the team management unfortunately saw little reason to change a formula that was working. They thought those who were complaining were just "do-gooders" and "troublemakers." They would bring a black player aboard when they felt the time was right—whatever that meant (it was never explained).

And now, it seemed, the time was right. The player's name was Elston Howard.

Howard was a catcher-outfielder who came from St. Louis, just like Yogi Berra. He had been a very good player in both the Negro Leagues and the International League. It was thought that either he or Vic Power would be the first black Yankee, but Power was considered too flashy, too much of a show-man, and he wound up traded to the Athletics. (The Yankees didn't really keep any flashy white players either—players who called attention to themselves and distracted from the game. Billy Martin was an exception.)

And so 1955 saw the debut of Howard, one of the finest gentlemen to ever play for the Yankees. While Jackie Robinson could be a little abrasive and not everyone on the team loved him, Ellie made friends easily.

Besides being a good guy, he was a perfect Stengel player. Casey could play him in the outfield or first base, or he could spell Berra at catcher. Eventually he would replace Berra as catcher. He was a smart baseball man and a leader on the field. He would later become the first African-American coach in the American League.

While Howard did not have the same problems that Robinson had in break-ing the color line, he did find things off the field to be challenging. Some neigh-bors objected when he tried to buy a home in New Jersey—but at the same time, others came forward to say that this was wrong, and that they wanted him here.

He also had problems in St. Petersburg, Florida, where the Yankees had spring training. Their hotel there did not want black guests and told the Yankees as much. Ellie had to find a place to stay in the "colored" section of town. It meant he couldn't be with his teammates over breakfast at the hotel, or couldn't con-veniently go out to dinner with them. Ellie's teammates didn't like him being excluded any more than he did. He was a very likable teammate.

Typically, the Yankees would play exhibition games on their way north to conclude each spring training, but that too came to a close in 1955, when too many of the cities they visited still had "colored only" sections in the stands or restricted the team in other ways so long as they had Howard on the team.

The Yankees stopped the traveling exhibitions after 1955 and put up with St. Petersburg's old-time Jim Crow laws for a few years—so long as they knew Ellie was well taken care of—but they knew it was wrong, and eventually they moved their spring headquarters to Fort Lauderdale, Florida, which did not impose the same restrictions. Fort Lauderdale was an up-and-coming city that made the Yankees a good offer to move, and the team jumped on it.

The Yankees were now an integrated ball club, and the days of all-white team photos were over. And they would be a better franchise for it.

By 1955 the era of Reynolds-Raschi-Lopat ended, leaving Ford as the team's ace for the rest of his career. Added to the pitching staff were hard-throwing Bob Turley and big Don Larsen, acquired in a seventeen-player trade with the Baltimore Orioles, the biggest in baseball history.

Cleveland was still tough in 1955 and beat the Yankees thirteen times in twenty-two games. It was the first season series the Yankees had lost to any team in seven years.

But led by Yogi Berra's third MVP season and eighteen wins from Ford, the Yankees got back into the World Series in '55 and again took on the Brooklyn Dodgers. They had beaten them in 1941, 1947, 1949, 1952, and 1953, and they were ready to beat them again.

Howard hit a home run his first time up in a World Series game, and the Yankees jumped off to a two-games-to-none lead. But the Dodgers were a great team—the "Boys of Summer" they were later called—and with a lineup featuring Jackie Robinson, Duke Snider, Gil Hodges, Roy Campanella, "Pee Wee" Reese, and more, they battled back. It came down to a seventh game, and this time the Dodgers won it. It was the first and only world championship in Brooklyn Dodgers history. The borough of Brooklyn celebrated with parties all over town, while the Yankees tried to put it behind them and set to work on recapturing the title. It was the professional thing to do—to go about business—and that was what the Yankees did best.

Losing to that great Dodgers team was no shame—beating them five times in six World Series was amazing. Still, it was a hard pill for Yankee fans to swallow. They just weren't used to losing.

CHAPTER 26

Triple Crown, Perfect Game

Four words covered the 1956 Yankees: triple crown, perfect game.

They were achievements for the ages.

Mickey Mantle led the American League in batting average, home runs, and runs batted in. This did not happen often, because home run hitters often don't hit for high averages, but in 1956, Mickey was the whole package. He hit fifty-two home runs, and for a while people were wondering if he might break Babe Ruth's record of sixty. Mantle pins, Mantle photos, even Mantle T-shirts sold briskly, long before baseball really knew about souvenir marketing.

Winning a triple crown was rare. Ted Williams had done it twice—in 1942 and 1947. Lou Gehrig had done it in 1934—the only other Yankee to accomplish it. Between 1967 and 2012, when Miguel Cabrera won it, no one had come close. It only proved how hard it was to do. Mick was the first switch-hitter to do it. He was already considered the greatest switch-hitter of all time.

Mick batted .353 and won his first Most Valuable Player award. He won almost every other award there was and was on the cover of every magazine, flashing that innocent toothy smile and winning the hearts of America as never before. A photographer named Ozzie Sweet had a special way of capturing Mantle looking especially heroic. He was all over television, with appearances on variety shows and commercials for soap, breakfast cereal, toothpaste, and cigarettes. Yes, this was before people knew the health dangers of smoking, and athletes often appeared in tobacco advertising, even if they didn't smoke! And Mickey didn't smoke.

He led the team back to the World Series and, to the players' delight, back against the Dodgers. The Yankees wanted revenge for losing in 1955.

Game five of the World Series, before a packed house on a sunny afternoon at Yankee Stadium, was everything you would want in a Series. Two great teams. American flags all over. People on the streets watching on TVs in the windows of electronic stores. People at work or even at school listening on portable radios. Some schools rolled television sets into classrooms. It was hard to get a good picture with "rabbit ears" antennas, but everyone did their best to make out the pictures.

Some people played hooky from school and went with their dads to the game. Joe Torre, who would eventually become the Yankees' manager, was only fifteen years old at the time and was there, rooting for his hometown Brooklyn Dodgers!

The Series was tied at two wins each. The Yankees chose Don Larsen to start. He learned of this when he got to the ballpark and saw a baseball in his shoe. That was Casey Stengel's way. He didn't always reveal the starter the day before—not even to the starter. He wanted to sleep on it.

Larsen was no star. He was actually a fairly ordinary pitcher. Sometimes good, sometimes bad. You never knew for sure what you were getting.

On this day, he was perfect.

Each inning he faced three Dodger hitters and retired them all. No base runners. No walks. No Yankee errors. When Larsen came to bat in the eighth inning, 64,519 fans stood and cheered—even the Dodger fans. Something special was going on here. Baseball history was being made.

Everyone knew what a no-hitter was, but not everyone knew what a perfect game was. There hadn't been one in the major leagues since 1922, and never one in the World Series. There had never been a no-hitter in the World Series either. A perfect game meant no runners. Every inning, three up, three down.

Artist Andy Jurinko painted the final pitch of Don Larsen's perfect game, with Billy Martin at second base and the scoreboard telling the story. (GoodSportsArt.com; copyright Andy Jurinko)

The Yankees scored two runs on a Mantle home run in the fourth inning, and then Mick made a great running catch in the fifth to save the possibility of the no-hitter. Of course, in the fifth inning, not everyone was thinking about a no-hitter. Or a perfect game. There was nothing in Larsen's history to suggest that this was possible.

In the ninth, the pressure on Larsen was tremendous. Larsen pitched without a windup, a style he had adopted just weeks before. The twenty-seventh batter for the Dodgers was a pinch hitter, Dale Mitchell. Larsen struck him out, and the place went crazy.

"A no-hitter, a perfect game!" screamed announcer Bob Wolff.

Yogi Berra, the catcher, ran out and jumped into Larsen's arms. This was not the end of the World Series, but it was the end of what came to be called the greatest game ever pitched. With everything at stake, with a national television audience, with a full Yankee Stadium on the biggest stage in sports, he had done it.

The Dodgers stayed alive with a 1–0 win the next day, but then young Johnny Kucks beat them 9–0 the day after, and the Yankees reclaimed the world championship. It would be Larsen's game that everyone would remember forever. Larsen was named Most Valuable Player of the World Series and received a new 1957 Corvette from *Sport* magazine.

CHAPTER 27

Trouble at the Copa

Phil "Scooter" Rizzuto was released during the 1956 season, and in 1957 he joined Mel Allen and Red Barber in the broadcast booth. He was actually released on Old-Timer's Day, going from active player to old-timer in an instant, and it hurt. But he went home, and on the advice of his old teammate Snuffy Stirnweiss, he didn't complain about how he'd been treated. It was smart. He got a broadcasting job.

He would continue to be a broadcaster until 1996, with his friendly style winning millions of admirers over the years. He rooted for the Yankees, of course—they had been paying him since 1941—but did it with such a fun style that even people who didn't root for the team would just say, "Oh, that's Scooter, that's the way he is." He called people huckleberries, he offered birthday greetings, he mentioned restaurants that he liked (and sometimes got his next meal there for free!), he exclaimed "Holy cow!" after a terrific play, he ate cannoli during the broadcasts, and sometimes he would be seen leaving a little early to beat the traffic. Yankee fans loved him as a player and as an announcer, and his career spanned fifty-six seasons, minus time spent in the navy during World War II.

For Phil Rizzuto, who broke in with Joe DiMaggio and retired from broadcasting during the era of Derek Jeter and Mariano Rivera, it was easy to look at his career and say, "Holy cow!"

For the most part, people expected broadcasters to call the game and leave their personal thoughts to themselves. For most of the history of baseball, at least until the 1970s, sportswriters also reported on the games and little else. If they wrote a story about a player, it would be about his family, his hunting and fishing, and his hopes for the season. It was understood that what he did on his own time was not going to be reported.

Somehow, people still knew that Babe Ruth ran around late at night, but that was where the line was drawn. Fans assumed that all their heroes may have had a beer after the game, but then went home and got a good night's sleep. They would wake up, have a bowl of Wheaties with milk, and head for the ballpark.

Of course, players didn't always do that. They were young men in their twenties, and they liked to enjoy a good time.

That was the case on May 29, 1957, when a bunch of players with their wives went out to celebrate Billy Martin's twenty-ninth birthday. They made a few stops along the way and wound up at the famous Copacabana nightclub in Manhattan. Mantle, Berra, Ford, Hank Bauer, Kucks, and of course Martin were there. Sammy Davis Jr. was the entertainer.

Things got a little out of hand. A heckler from a bowling team, seated nearby, was yelling racial insults at Sammy Davis Jr., who was African-American.

Bauer, a tough old Marine, told them to shut up. They didn't.

One thing led to another, Bauer followed the heckler into the men's room, and the next thing anyone knew, the heckler was semiconscious on the floor and the Yankee players and their wives were being led out the back door into the night.

This one couldn't be ignored by the newspapers. It was a huge story. Even though Bauer had been defending Davis, the fact that this story was such big news bothered the front office a lot. A player acting violently in public wasn't good for the team's image.

George Weiss decided it was time to get rid of Billy Martin, whom he considered a bad influence on Mantle and a troublemaker. Weiss figured that eventually, Martin was going to get Mantle into trouble. Bringing him to the Copa reminded him of the risk. Things happened with Billy, even under the best of circumstances, like celebrating his birthday. In many ways, Billy was the heart and soul of the team, the scrappy infielder who played over his abilities in big situations.

A magazine once described ex-Marine Hank Bauer as having a face that looked like a clenched fist.
He had a seventeen-game hitting streak in World Series play. (Rogers Photo Archives)

But the Yankees had a talented replacement ready named Bobby Richardson, and Weiss was firm. Martin was traded to Kansas City. Casey Stengel, who loved Billy (and who didn't really love "milkshake drinkers" who never drank alcohol, like Richardson), was unable to stop the trade.

Billy went to Casey's office. "Casey, can't you do anything? Please?"

There was nothing that could be done. Casey had nothing to say to him.

Billy was deeply hurt. He cried. And he didn't speak to Stengel for years. He was never the same player again, because all he had ever wanted to be was a Yankee.

Billy and Casey finally patched things up late in Casey's life, as though nothing had happened. When Casey died in 1975, Billy was the only Yankee at his funeral, and the only one to wear a black armband in Casey's honor the following year.

With Billy traded, Mantle hit a career high of .365 in 1957 and won his second straight MVP award, but his home runs fell to thirty-four, and Weiss tried to cut his salary after the season. After hitting .365! Mick held out as long as he could, finally signing for a small raise to $75,000, but these were the days before players held open the possibility of one day becoming free agents and leaving. They had to take what was offered. For years Mantle would tell this story to people—Weiss trying to cut his salary after he hit .365.

Weiss knew he had a great star on his team; he just tried to sign him for as little money as possible. Mick would remain a Yankee for the rest of his career.

CHAPTER 28

The Milwaukee World Series

Bobby Richardson wasn't the only rookie on the '57 Yankees—Tony Kubek was there too. The two of them had played second base and shortstop together at Denver, the Yankees' top farm team, the year before. Ralph Houk was their manager.

Richardson, from South Carolina, was a very religious man who became active in establishing the Fellowship of Christian Athletes and the Baseball Chapel. Kubek, from Milwaukee, was quiet and shy and didn't care very much to do interviews. Few would have thought that he would one day be an outspoken star network broadcaster who would eventually win the Ford Frick Award for his broadcast work and be honored at the Baseball Hall of Fame.

George Weiss once hired a private detective to follow them on the road to make sure they weren't getting into any Billy Martin–like trouble. The detective reported that they had a night playing Ping-Pong at a local YMCA.

Kubek was Rookie of the Year in 1957, and it seemed fitting that he would play his first World Series in his hometown of Milwaukee in front of many friends and relatives. And he answered the call by hitting two home runs in game three in front of those very people.

The Braves had moved to Milwaukee in 1953, leaving Boston and beginning the movement of teams to places where they could draw more people and make more money. There had not been a change to major league's geography since the Yankees were formed in 1903 to replace Baltimore. The St. Louis Browns became the Baltimore Orioles in 1954, and the Philadelphia Athletics became the Kansas City Athletics in 1955. (The Braves later moved to Atlanta, the Athletics to Oakland.)

Bobby Richardson, here receiving an award from the Salvation Army, was often a World Series hero.
(Rogers Photo Archives)

The year 1957 would be the last for the Brooklyn Dodgers and New York Giants, who would move to Los Angeles and San Francisco respectively, continuing the pattern started by the Braves. The Yankees would have New York all to themselves.

As for the World Series, the Yankees and Braves were tied 3–3, forcing a game seven, and the Braves sent Lew Burdette to the mound. Burdette, once a Yankee farmhand, had beaten the Yankees twice already. And he did it again, winning 5–0 and becoming only the third pitcher in history to win three games in a World Series.

The Yankees again won the pennant in 1958, and again faced the Braves in the Series. This was still a mighty Braves team, with Hank Aaron and Eddie Mathews in the lineup, and with Warren Spahn on the mound. And the Braves jumped off to a 3–1 lead, apparently headed for back-to-back titles. It looked bad for the Yankees. Very bad.

But the Yankees' best weapon that year was "Bullet Bob" Turley, the hard-throwing right-hander who had come to New York in the same trade as Larsen

"Bullet Bob" Turley was the hero of the 1958 comeback victory in the World Series against Milwaukee.
(Rogers Photo Archives)

four years before. Bob had a magical season in 1958, winning twenty-one games and the Cy Young Award as the major leagues' best pitcher. (This was before each league had its own winner.)

Now Turley pitched a complete game shutout to win game five, got a tenth-inning save in the Yankees' sixth-game win, and pitched six and two-thirds innings of relief to get the win in game seven, making him the Most Valuable Player of the World Series (and he got a Corvette, too!). The Yankees had overcome being down 3–1 and had won their eighteenth world championship.

For those who played through the Casey Stengel years, or those who worked in the front office, no championship was as satisfying as this one. From being down three games to one and facing a second straight loss to the Braves, coming back and playing like the Yankees of old meant a lot to those players.

CHAPTER 29

Finding Roger Maris

So high were expectations for the Yankees each year that when they fell to last place on May 20, 1959, headlines all over the country screamed YANKEES HIT CELLAR! It wasn't the Yankees' best year, to be sure, but they did finish third, and it was unrealistic to expect to win all the time.

Near the end of the season, Kansas City manager Harry Craft walked over to Stengel during batting practice and pointed to Roger Maris, his right fielder.

"You guys ought to try and get him this winter," said Craft. "He's really a terrific player."

Craft had played in the minor leagues for the Yankees and was Mickey Mantle's first minor league manager. He knew his days were numbered as Kansas City manager, so he thought he'd pass along the tip.

The Yankees were probably thinking about Maris anyway. They had a cozy relationship with the Kansas City Athletics and always seemed to be making trades with them to get their best players. There was a lot of business going on between the two clubs, involving real estate, loans, and personnel. The Athletics management had very close business ties to the Yankee owners, Dan Topping and Del Webb.

Maris was not widely known outside of Kansas City, although he had also played for Cleveland. A native of Fargo, North Dakota, he liked it that way. He was not a big city guy, and didn't like the fast pace of New York. He had settled near Kansas City with his family and seemed perfectly happy to play in that small town. But in 1959 there would be nothing he could do about being traded; he just had to go where he was sent.

The Yankees and Athletics made a seven-player deal that brought Maris to New York. They gave up Hank Bauer, the popular but aging right fielder who Maris would replace, along with Don Larsen. That was just good baseball business—move an older player out, get a younger player in. Maris was only twenty-five; Bauer was thirty-seven. (Bauer would become the Athletics' manager.)

Maris also had a great swing for Yankee Stadium. Power hitting left-hand batters loved the "short porch" in right field, which went back to Babe Ruth and whose dimensions had made the stadium known as "the House that Ruth Built."

Maris not only made the adjustment to New York, he became a star. He led the league in runs batted in, belted thirty-nine home runs, and won a Gold Glove in right field, showing great range and a strong throwing arm. Because he batted in front of Mantle in the lineup, the two started to be called "the M&M Boys." In Roger's first season with the Yankees, 1960, he gave Stengel an MVP award-winning season, beating out Mantle by a narrow margin.

Even with Maris on board, the Yankees had to struggle a bit to win the pennant in 1960, fighting off a talented young Baltimore Orioles team—but win it they did, for the tenth time in Stengel's twelve years as manager.

And now they would face the Pittsburgh Pirates in the World Series. It was the first pennant for the Pirates since 1925, when "Murderers' Row" took them down in four straight. The 1960 Series would be remembered for three Yankee blowout victories (10–0, 12–0 and 16–3), and an epic game seven at Forbes Field in Pittsburgh.

The lead kept changing hands. With each home run, it looked like a new hero was ready for the history books (and his Corvette). One was Yogi Berra; another was Bill "Moose" Skowron, the Yankees' power-hitting first baseman. (He wasn't called Moose because he looked like a moose, but because as a baby, his father thought he looked like the Italian World War II dictator Benito Mussolini.) Another still was the Pirates' Hal Smith, long ago a Yankee farmhand who, like many other catchers in the Yankee system, got traded away because Yogi was just too good.

In the last of the eighth, the Yankees had a 7–4 lead and were looking good. But a potential double-play grounder to Kubek at short hit a pebble, took a bad bounce, and got Tony in the throat. It knocked him down, and everybody was safe. Kubek had to go to the hospital, and the Pirates rallied for five runs and had a 9–7 lead.

But what a game! And the Yankees were not done. They tied it in the top of the ninth with their backs to the wall, and now it was 9–9, last of the ninth, seventh game. Oh boy!

In to pitch for the Yanks came Ralph Terry, a young right-hander who, like Maris, had come to New York from Kansas City in 1959. The first batter was Bill Mazeroski, a great fielding second baseman not especially known for his hitting. But on Terry's second pitch, Maz swung and drove the ball over the left field wall—the most famous hit in Pittsburgh history, a world championship home run. The Yankees, despite outscoring the Pirates 55–27 in the seven games, lost. Despite Richardson hitting a grand slam home run, driving in a record twelve runs, and winning the Series MVP award (his Corvette!), the Yankees lost. (Bobby is the only losing player to ever win the award.)

The Yankees, despite Whitey Ford breaking Babe Ruth's pitching record (when Ruth was with Boston) for consecutive scoreless innings, lost.

In the clubhouse, Mantle was not the only player in tears. Many were. Players play hard and give their all to make it to the World Series. It didn't matter how many they had already won. This was a tough loss.

Five days after the World Series, the Yankees fired Casey Stengel. He was blamed hard for this World Series loss—blamed in particular for not starting Ford in game one so that he might be available to make three starts, including a potential game seven. Ford's two shutouts against the Pirates only highlighted the "mistake" that people thought Casey had made. But mostly, the Yankees felt Casey's time had passed; age had caught up with him.

Fans and the press, however, were outraged. They felt that firing Casey Stengel after losing the seventh game of the World Series, after winning ten pennants in twelve years, was completely unfair.

But baseball could be a cruel business, and Casey was out. So too was George Weiss, moved to an "advisory" position. A new era was coming.

CHAPTER 30

The Great Home Run Race

The Yankees wouldn't be without a manager for long, though. Waiting in the wings was the first-base coach, Ralph Houk, who had managed for them in the minor leagues. In naming Houk as their new manager, the Yankees were hoping that the fans would love the rather unknown new man as soon as the team did what they always did—win.

Houk had been a US Marine and decorated combat veteran in World War II and was a real leader of men. Yankee players loved him almost immediately. "We'd run through a wall for Ralph Houk," was said often.

He had a great roster, but he did some things differently from Casey. First, he called Mantle in and said, "You're my leader. We don't have a captain on this team, but on the field, you are the guy everyone respects." (The team had "retired" the captain position after Lou Gehrig died.)

It made Mantle take more responsibility, as he approached his eleventh season with the team.

He called Whitey Ford in and said, "You're my starting pitcher every fourth day. No more of this shuffling the rotation until it's a good time for your turn."

Whitey went out and won twenty games for the first time in his career, and the Cy Young Award with it. He was an amazing 25–4.

Houk made Luis Arroyo into an outstanding relief pitcher who won fifteen games and saved twenty-nine that year, long before the word "closer" was ever used.

He moved Yogi to left field and made Ellie Howard the number one catcher. Yogi, Ellie, and John Blanchard were listed on the roster as catchers, and the three of them combined for sixty home runs.

The team hit a major league record of 240 homers.

It seemed everything Ralph Houk did worked!

The year 1961 began with two new teams—the Los Angeles Angels and the (new) Washington Senators (the old ones became the Minnesota Twins)—and an expanded schedule. Eight games were added, to make a 162-game season.

The additional eight games had some writers asking, "Sixty-one homers in '61?" By June, those spring training stories began to get real. Mantle and Maris—the M&M Boys—were staging an epic battle to break Ruth's home run record of sixty. Could they do it? Everyone was talking about it.

Mantle was enjoying it. Relaxed in his new role, he was almost amused by how tough the writers were on Maris, asking him day after day, "Do you think you'll hit sixty-one?"

Roger's patience was growing thin. He wasn't enjoying all the attention and speculation. He thought the writers were asking a stupid, impossible-to-answer question, and he grew grumpy over it. Mantle, asked the same questions, learned to give easy answers and smile.

In the summer, the commissioner, Ford Frick, ruled that if the record—or any record—fell *after* the 154th game, it would be listed separately in the record books. It wouldn't have an asterisk—it would have a separate listing altogether—but everyone began calling the decision "the asterisk ruling."

Frick was in a jam. The extra games could make all the old records go away. It didn't help him any that he had once been a friend of Ruth's, and when he was a sportswriter, he was often Ruth's "ghostwriter," writing "by Babe Ruth" stories for him.

This was still a time when baseball cherished the old more than the new. They were still promoting the great names from the past instead of the great new players. They were missing the boat. Everyone was talking about Maris and Mantle!

On went the summer, Mantle and Maris racing toward sixty, and all attention on them. Maris, it was reported, was losing clumps of hair from worrying. They were said to be feuding, but actually, they were becoming great friends and even shared an apartment.

The fans were rooting for Mantle—and even booing Maris! Maris was thought to be "unworthy"—not really a Yankee, too young, not friendly enough. Not enough years with the Yankees. Mickey by now had earned the right. He had always been a popular player and a star for the Yankees. He was the much more obvious player to root for.

Even old-time players were lining up, supporting Babe's record—even Mrs. Babe Ruth. It was the culture of many in the game to support the old records and the old stars, and not to root hard for records to fall.

Most people agreed that September would kill their chances anyway, for Babe had hit seventeen that month. With all the pressure, it would be quite a feat to hit that many to catch the Babe.

Mantle entered September with forty-eight, Maris with fifty-one. They wouldn't need seventeen. It looked like it could happen!

But Mantle was injured and never got there. He wound up with fifty-four, his career best. What a run he had given it! And the fans fell in love with him as never before. From that time forward, through the remaining seven years of his career, Mickey was the most popular player in baseball—at home and on the road, no longer booed, and always appreciated and cheered. Earlier in his career, when he didn't seem to be as good as DiMaggio, fans booed him, especially when he struck out. Now that was fading away forever.

Now Maris was trying to get to sixty by the 154th game to at least tie the

Babe. Entering the game he had fifty-eight, and he hit one—but not two.

Thanks to Frick's ruling, a lot of people lost interest in the chase. It was a shame—it should have been a great time for baseball, with enthusiasm never higher! Roger hit his sixtieth in game 159—but in game 162, his last chance, only 23,154 were in Yankee Stadium, most of them in right field, hoping to catch the ball. A restaurant owner had offered a five-thousand-dollar reward for the ball.

The nation was focused on the home run race of 1961 between the "M&M Boys"—Mickey Mantle (left) and Roger Maris. (Ozzie Sweet photo; courtesy of Randall Swearingen)

Roger came through. Under all that pressure, he delivered number sixty-one off Boston's Tracy Stallard. He did it! (Nineteen-year-old Sal Durante from Brooklyn, later a school bus driver, caught the ball and got the reward, using the money to get married.)

And after more than fifty years, it is still in the books as the American League record, even if some National Leaguers have broken it, possibly with the aid of steroids or other performance-enhancing drugs.

If anyone needed an asterisk, it wasn't Roger Maris. (Some thirty years later, the so-called asterisk was removed by Commissioner Fay Vincent. And forty years later, Billy Crystal made a movie about the season called *61*.*)

Roger won his second straight MVP award and got to visit President Kennedy in the White House.

But it didn't give him joy. He simply wasn't a fan of the spotlight.

The '61 Yankees were often compared to the Murderers' Row Yankees of 1927. They were that good. And after winning 109 games in the regular season, they beat Cincinnati in five games and won the World Series.

Three Brash Rookies

That corporate Yankee style, that "look," those unwritten rules that said "Yankees must conform and behave like Yankees," took a hit in 1962. While the Yankees had always made a point to bring in a certain type of "behave yourself, don't challenge the rules" players (with Babe Ruth and Billy Martin the noted exceptions), the '62 season saw three untraditional players join the team.

Actually, there were four new faces, but one of them, Tom Tresh, was very much a Yankee of old. He and another rookie, Phil Linz, came up to compete for the shortstop job while Kubek was off on army duty. Tresh won the job, and later moved to left field when Kubek returned. He even won the Rookie of the Year award.

Linz became a utility player with a big sense of humor, a "supersub," a guy who was good for a laugh and was happy to be in the major leagues no matter what his role. "Play me or keep me," was his motto, an answer to most bench players who would say, "Play me or trade me!"

Jim Bouton was a rookie pitcher who had been a big baseball fan as a kid growing up in New Jersey. This was unusual, because most players weren't fans.

They were too busy playing the game to learn about it like most fans do. He had ideas that were not like the typical players, who lived very conservative lives, obeyed coaches, and accepted long-held beliefs without question. Jim always questioned things, especially authority. He was tough on the mound, though—he was known as "Bulldog" Jim Bouton, and his right arm came so over the top when he delivered that it would knock his cap off.

Bouton achieved his greatest fame about eight years later when his career ended and he published a very funny memoir called *Ball Four*. It was a bestseller, and through reading it, a lot of people fell in love with baseball, laughing at his stories. But many in baseball felt he was telling tales from the clubhouse that shouldn't have been told—that he should have followed the code of the clubhouse: "What is said here, stays here." As a result, Jim was seldom welcome at old-timers' gatherings, even though he became a twenty-game winner with the Yankees and a World Series star.

And then there was Joe Pepitone, who came from the streets of Brooklyn. He had a certain swagger to his style. He would be the first Yankee to use a hair dryer to get his look "just right" after games. And he had a lot of pop in his bat, which was perfect for Yankee Stadium. As an Italian American, he hoped people would think of him with Lazzeri-DiMaggio-Crosetti-Rizzuto-Berra. But although he enjoyed some good seasons, he never realized his full potential. When he wrote his autobiography years later, he called it *Joe, You Could Have Made Us Proud*.

Meanwhile, there was news across the Harlem River, back in the old Polo Grounds where the Yankees (and of course the Giants) had played. After four years without National League baseball in town, New York was getting a new team called the Mets. And they'd hired Casey Stengel to manage them and George Weiss to be the general manager!

This proved to be a brilliant decision by the new owners of the Mets. Although the Mets were an awful team, losing 120 out of 160 in 1962, their first year, the writers loved Stengel, and he did a lot to deflect attention away from the bad play

Joe Pepitone (left) and Tom Tresh both burst onto the scene in 1962—two of four rookies to make the club that year. (Rogers Photo Archives)

and onto himself. Much of what he did helped win a lot of old Dodgers and Giants fans to the Mets in a hurry. And as the team got ready to move into a new ballpark in Queens called Shea Stadium in 1964, they were out to prove that they could be good competition to the Yankees for the hearts of New York's baseball fans.

Mets fans seemed louder, younger, more fun-loving, more playful. The Yankee fans were certainly more serious. While Mets fans started painting sayings on bedsheets and bringing banners to games, the Yankees forbid it, saying they would block the view of other fans. Blocking the view might have been what the Mets were trying to accomplish, since they lost so much!

One of the original Mets was the one-time Yankee outfielder Gene Woodling. He had been part of the five straight world championships under Stengel from 1949 to 1953. Now he was watching his new team find new ways to lose every day.

One day he was sitting on the bench when Casey walked by. They looked at each other. Casey winked and said, "Ain't like the old days, is it?" And they both laughed. It sure wasn't.

The Yankees won the 1962 pennant, with Richardson collecting 209 hits, and although Mantle won his third MVP award, he said, "It should have gone to Bobby." The World Series would find them facing the San Francisco Giants, and what a Series it was.

It went down to the ninth inning of the seventh game, just as the 1960 World Series had done when Mazeroski had homered off Terry.

Now Terry was on the mound again with a 1–0 lead. A rare chance at redemption on the biggest sports stage in America.

The Yankees had scored their run on a double-play grounder. Terry had allowed only two hits. Matty Alou was on third, and Willie Mays was on second with two out. Alou had to hold at third when Maris made a great throw from right field on Willie's double. Maris had fallen to only thirty-three home runs in 1962, but he was still a clutch hitter, and still a great outfielder.

Up came the left-hand-hitting Willie McCovey, a great slugger and future MVP and Hall of Famer. What a moment! A single could drive in two and give the Giants the World Series. Losing to winning in one swing!

But instead of a single, McCovey ripped a hard liner that Richardson was able to grab as he moved to his left, before it got to the outfield. Another few inches and it would have been a base hit. Instead the Yankees won 1–0, and Terry was carried off the field by his teammates, a hero!

It was their twentieth world championship—and their last for fifteen years. No one knew it at the time, of course.

For 1963, the Yankees brought up left-hander Al Downing, their first African-American pitcher, and he came through with a 13–5 record. Ford and Bouton both won more than twenty games, and Elston Howard won the league's Most Valuable Player award with a terrific season both at bat and in handling the pitching staff. Ellie had long been a very valuable Yankee, but now he was recognized by all for his contributions.

After losing the seventh game of the 1960 World Series, Ralph Terry is carried off the field upon winning the seventh game in 1962. (Rogers Photo Archives)

For Ralph Houk, it was three pennants in his first three years, an accomplishment that made baseball history. Any lingering doubts about letting Casey go after 1960 had long faded. "The Major" (his rank in World War II) was now considered one of the best managers in baseball.

In the days before one or two rounds of play-offs, the regular season would lead right into the World Series, and if both pennant winners had a few days to rest their regulars, they could create a situation in which their best starting pitchers could go head-to-head in games one, four, and seven.

So baseball's attention turned to game one at Yankee Stadium, the 1963 World Series, and the matchup everyone was hoping for—the Yankees' Whitey Ford against the Dodgers' Sandy Koufax. Here were two guys, the best left-handers in the business, Ford born in Queens, Koufax in Brooklyn, both at the top of their game.

"Pitching in Yankee Stadium feels like pitching in the Grand Canyon," said Koufax, who had been with the Dodgers for the 1955 and 1956 World Series but had not gotten into any games. He was a player who came to be revered by all fans of baseball as the best pitcher of his time. Even Yankee fans had to admire him greatly.

Koufax's reputation for throwing hard was known to all. But as the game moved forward, Yankee fans sat in their seats silently, watching a master at work. Koufax set a record with fifteen strikeouts in a World Series game, even getting Richardson three times. And Bobby hardly ever struck out! It was the performance of a lifetime, and it set the stage for the Dodgers winning in four straight, a first for the Yankees and an embarrassing setback for the proud team.

But change was coming.

CHAPTER 32

Manager Berra

General Manager Roy Hamey, Weiss's successor, retired, and Houk, after so many years in uniform as a catcher, coach, and manager, was going to the front office to be his replacement.

And the new manager was to be Yogi Berra.

Yogi had been first-base coach in 1963 but was still available at age thirty-eight to pinch-hit and catch a little. Now he would retire after eighteen Yankee seasons and become the manager of the defending American League champions.

Everyone knew Yogi was a genius at his craft. Casey had long called him "my assistant manager." But this was a tall order. He was never considered a great communicator, but rather someone who just did things he knew to be right. He never could explain, for instance, his ability to keep the ball in play and not strike out very often. "You just hit it," he'd say.

Even putting aside his communication issues—and he would have to talk to the press every day—it was not easy to ask a man to manage the fellows who had been his teammates. He was going to be the "boss" of Mantle, Maris, Ford, Howard, Kubek, Richardson, Clete Boyer, Johnny Blanchard—all the guys he had played with and gone to dinner with for years. This was a lot to ask of anyone, even someone as admired as Yogi was.

And Houk, his onetime backup catcher, was going to be his boss.

Yogi named Ford to be his pitching coach, while Ford continued to play and be the ace of the pitching staff. The 1964 season was a struggle—winning did not come easily. By the middle of August, the team was in third place, and everyone was ready to blame Yogi. Then they called up their best minor league pitcher, a tall, thin right-hander named Mel Stottlemyre, to join the rotation. The move would save the season.

On August 12, Mel made his debut and beat the Chicago White Sox 7–3, aided by one of the longest home runs of Mantle's career, a drive to dead center field in Yankee Stadium, over the "batter's eye" black screen that gave hitters a clearer view of the pitch. For years there had been no "batter's eye" in baseball, and fans in white or colored shirts sitting in center would make seeing a pitch extra difficult for hitters. It was a safety issue, and finally ballparks began to raise black screens to reduce the danger of not seeing a pitch.

Mel was off to a 9–3 record for the remaining six weeks of the season, a debut that for many recalled Whitey Ford's 9–1 debut in 1950. He was a master of the sinker ball, which resulted in many ground balls being hit. Often with Mel, you knew in the first inning if his sinker was working that day. If hitters were grounding out, he was "on." Even if they were hitting grounders for base hits through the infield, you knew he was on. He would wind up pitching forty shutouts in his career and would be one of the greatest pitchers in Yankee history. But the 1964 World Series was the only one in which he ever pitched.

The days of the season were starting to wind down. The heat was on Yogi. The Yankees had won four straight pennants, but there was no room for error with this team. Finishing first was always the mission.

The Yankees were in Chicago. They had lost four in a row, sitting in third place and feeling pennant hopes slipping away. As was always the case after a loss, the team dressed in silence, and one by one got on the team bus outside the ballpark, ready to head for the airport.

In the back of the bus, utility infielder Phil Linz pulled out his new harmonica. He had just been learning how to use it, and he started to play "Mary Had a Little Lamb."

Innocent though he might have been, it just wasn't the code of conduct after a loss. Things were supposed to be quiet. And Yogi's nerves were on edge.

"Shut that thing up," he yelled from his front-row seat. The managers always sat in the first row.

Linz asked, "What did he say?"

Mantle, not thinking that this was such a serious moment, had fun with it.

"He said play it louder," he replied. And Phil did.

Yogi got up from his seat, walked to the back of the bus, and slapped the harmonica out of Linz's hands.

"I said put it away," said Yogi. "You'd think we just *won* four games."

When he slapped the harmonica out of Linz's hands, it careened off Joe Pepitone's knee.

"Oh, I'm hurt," said Pepitone. But he was joking too. Somehow, he thought it was all part of a funny moment.

It was anything but.

The team headed for Boston. The writers in the bus saw what happened. It was the story of the day. Yogi fined Linz two hundred dollars. Linz was making a $14,000 salary and counting on a World Series share, so two hundred dollars was a big fine. In those days, fines were sometimes as little as fifty dollars.

The Yankees lost their next two in Boston but then won seven of their next nine. They were playing better. They were playing like Yankees. The writers began to report that the harmonica incident had woken up the club, had given Yogi a chance to show leadership, and had reminded them of the professional way they were supposed to behave.

Veteran pitcher Pedro Ramos joined the team on September 5. He saved

Manager Yogi Berra (center) with two late-season arrivals who helped win the 1964 pennant for the Yankees—Mel Stottlemyre (left) and Pedro Ramos (right). (Rogers Photo Archives)

eight games down the stretch. He was a big hit with the fans, a fun guy to have on the team. He and Stottlemyre turned the pitching staff around. And the Yankees won their twenty-ninth pennant by one game. It was their fifth pennant in a row.

And it was a close call.

Now the Yankees faced the St. Louis Cardinals in the World Series. Their manager, Johnny Keane, had been rumored to be fired all during September, but the Cardinals held on, kept winning, and beat out the Philadelphia Phillies to shock everyone and win the pennant. The Phillies had a big lead but blew it.

This was a tight series. In game three, Mantle homered off knuckleball relief pitcher Barney Schultz in the last of the ninth for a World Series walk-off homer, the sixteenth home run of his World Series career, breaking a tie with Babe Ruth for first place. (He would hit two more for eighteen.)

Jim Bouton won the Mantle walkoff game and game six. Now there would be a game seven. The Yankees had not lost two World Series in a row since their first two, 1921 and 1922. Game seven would be the great Bob Gibson against the rookie ace, Stottlemyre.

Gibson wasn't his usual dominating self, and even Linz managed to hit a home run against him. But he made pitches when he had to, and he held on for a tough 7–5 win to give the Cards the world championship.

From St. Louis, where the World Series had ended, the Yankees' public relations director, Bob Fishel, was told by Houk to call a press conference for the very next day back in New York.

And in a Fifth Avenue hotel ballroom across the street from the Yankee offices, in the same place where the Yankees had fired Stengel four years earlier, they fired Yogi Berra. The decision was made by Houk. It was a shock, even with the rumors. After all, he had won the pennant in his first year as manager, went to the seventh game of the World Series, and was one of the most popular sports heroes ever in New York. But all that didn't seem to matter much when the Yankees couldn't win the World Series. He was gone.

Yogi wouldn't be out of a job, though. The Mets would hire him as a coach for the following season. (And he would later become the Mets' manager, win another pennant, and lose another seven-game World Series in 1973.)

To further shock the sports world, Johnny Keane quit as manager of the Cardinals—and immediately signed with the Yankees. Keane had resented the way he had been treated by Cardinals management when the team looked like it would not win. When they did win, he showed them all by quitting—and taking the Yankees job. What a turnaround!

In August, Topping and Webb sold the Yankees to CBS.

The television network would be the first network to buy a major league team, and many wondered what it would mean. For now, it meant nothing. Topping and Webb insisted that Yogi's firing and Keane's hiring had not been ordered by CBS.

And yet, another big change made this all just a continuing series of strange events. Yankees broadcaster Mel Allen was fired! The Voice of the Yankees was told that his broadcasting days, at least with the Yankees, were over.

For Yankee fans who associated his voice with the team, this was unthinkable. What had happened? Mel was only fifty-one—he wasn't retiring.

The Yankees never gave a reason, other than "it's time for a change." They never even gave Mel a reason. He would go on to be the voice of *This Week in Baseball*, and would later come back and do cable broadcasts for the Yankees, but being fired broke his heart and left Yankee fans bewildered. Rumors circled, but nothing was ever said by the Yankees, not a word.

So no Yogi, no Mel, no Topping-Webb ownership, and an uncertain future for sure.

CHAPTER 33

The Dynasty Crumbles

The Yankees dynasty collapsed in 1965. After twenty-nine pennants in forty-four years, including the last five in a row and fourteen in the last seventeen, the team tumbled into fifth place—the second division. It was a shock, unless you dug deeply to find out the combination of reasons.

None of them were superstitions.

Topping and Webb selling the team was part of the reason. CBS did nothing wrong in that first year, but suddenly it became apparent that Topping and Webb were probably planning on selling for several years and had allowed the farm system to "dry up." After the four rookies in 1962—Pepitone, Tresh, Linz, and Bouton—and after Al Downing in 1963 and Stottlemyre in 1964, there was not much left in the minor leagues that looked like big-time talent. Some rookies would emerge over the next few years—Horace Clarke, Fritz Peterson, Roy White, and Bobby Murcer—who would be major-league-caliber players, but the stars on the level of DiMaggio and Mantle and Berra were not to be found.

Of course this was a problem for all of baseball, not just for the Yankees. The NFL was getting bigger all the time, and the NBA was coming on strong. Great athletes in high schools and colleges who played baseball and other sports were starting to choose other sports. Those sports were getting glamorous. Baseball still required minor-league seasoning, but if you thought of yourself as a "star" in football or basketball, you could go right to the NFL or NBA out of college.

Additionally, the American League had fallen way behind the National League in signing African-American players. The National League got Jackie Robinson and followed him with Willie Mays, Roy Campanella, Hank Aaron, Ernie Banks, Frank Robinson, Bob Gibson, Lou Brock, and many others. Dark-skinned Latin players like Roberto Clemente and Orlando Cepeda were picking National League teams. The American League was lagging behind in diversity, and it showed.

In 1965 baseball created an annual "draft" of high school and college players, which would eliminate the Yankees' advantage in signing whoever they wanted to. Now teams would select players based on where they finished in the standings, one round at a time, with the worst team picking first. The Yankees, used to finishing first, would not have the top choices. Still, this was not the cause for the collapse in 1965, as it would take several years for the new system to have an effect.

So with great players choosing other sports, the draft system in place, and with most African-American and Latino players choosing National League teams, the Yankees were suddenly on level ground with their American League opponents. They were losing their edge. They couldn't just go out and find "the next Mickey Mantle," who would jump at the chance to sign with the Yankees. "The next Mickey Mantle" might choose to play in the NFL. He might see the diversity of the National League and choose to play for one of their clubs. Or he might get drafted first by a team seeded lower than the Yankees.

Mantle himself—the real one, not the next one—was slowing down. Although he was only thirty-two in 1964, that was his last big season. He would play four more years, but they were very ordinary by Mantle standards. He may have been the most popular player in the game, but fans were cheering the memories, not what was really going on.

Other players were slowing down, getting old. Whitey Ford was one. He would retire in 1967. Tony Kubek, the shortstop, and Bobby Richardson, the second baseman, would retire in 1965 and 1966 respectively. They were young, and to lose players without getting anything in return was not the way the Yankees were used to operating. Few players ever retired. The Yankees would have preferred to trade them for younger players, but once they said they were retiring, there went any chance of doing that!

Roger Maris was hurting, and he was angry with the Yankees for not being direct with him about a hand injury. The team felt they were better off having him play through the injury than come out of the lineup. He felt they were making him play when they knew he couldn't swing the bat well. He was eventually traded to the Cardinals, and they didn't get much in return.

There was one promising trade on the horizon: the great fielding Yankees third baseman, Clete Boyer, would go to the Braves in exchange for a young outfield prospect named Bill Robinson. Robinson was African American and seemed to have the skills to be a big star. But he failed to make the grade with the Yankees and went on to have good seasons in the National League instead.

The new president of the Yankees—the man chosen to run the team for CBS—was named Michael Burke. He was not a baseball man, but he did bring in Lee MacPhail to be general manager. Lee—the son of Larry MacPhail, the one-time owner—was a fine baseball man, but his timing was bad. He couldn't reverse the falling fortunes of the Yankees at all.

On the field, the hiring of Johnny Keane as manager was a flop. He was not used to this veteran team whose players liked to make their own rules and were used to relaxed rules under Houk and Berra. He tried to bring discipline to the job but wasn't successful. He was also uninspiring. The players did not respond well to his leadership. He was fired a month into his second season, when it looked like another bad finish was developing.

Attendance at Yankee Stadium was falling, of course. Yankee fans liked winners. To counter the decline, the Yankees began staging promotion days—like

Bat Day and Cap Day. The team had been reluctant to do such things while they were winning, feeling that good baseball was enough. But it wasn't anymore, and they knew it. Promotion days were here to stay, which, for the fans at least, was a good thing.

On September 22, 1966, a makeup game on a rainy, miserable day in the Bronx drew 413 fans—413! It was hard to believe. Announcer Red Barber made the mistake of asking his director to show the empty stands (he was trying to be a good reporter), and he was fired soon after the season ended.

The Yankees fired Johnny Keane after losing sixteen of their first twenty games in 1966 and replaced him with Houk. Houk moved down from the front office, put on the uniform again, and tried to revive the team. But it was too late. All those bad things were in place. This team was going to finish last for only its second time in history. and Houk's reputation was going down with it.

Johnny Keane died eight months after being fired. He had a heart attack, but some wrote that he died of a broken heart. He had certainly come along at a bad time.

Meanwhile, while the Yankees stumbled along, fans of other teams were rejoicing. They had gone into every season hoping to finish second behind the Yankees. Now it was their turn at last. The Yankees were not going to be in the way. And so one by one, the Twins, the Orioles, the Red Sox, the Tigers, and the Athletics took turns going to the World Series, thrilling their hometown fans and opening up the pennant races at last. And for people who hated the Yankees—oh, this was a long time coming. They couldn't be happier!

CHAPTER 34

The Horace Clarke Years

Horace Clarke wasn't really the problem during these lean years. The second baseman from the Virgin Islands was by some measures above average. He had good speed, he had a decent average for an infielder, and his fielding was unspectacular but efficient. The problem was, he was the kind of second base-man who you would find on teams that didn't win pennants—pretty ordinary. And year after year, there he was. The Yankees could not seem to find anyone better. So the whole period of the Yankees' decline, which lasted from 1965 to 1975, came to be called "the Horace Clarke Era." It would be nice to have a whole era named after you—but it was meant to be insulting. It meant . . . very ordinary.

It might also have been the Fritz Peterson Era, but the honor stayed with Clarke. Fritz was a twenty-game winner and an All-Star, but he was a ground-ball pitcher like Stottlemyre, and he happened to pitch for a team without star infielders to make great plays behind him.

Elston Howard's time as a Yankee came to a close in 1967. The first African-American Yankee had taken his place with Dickey and Berra in the line of great

Horace Clarke had a whole Yankee era named for him, but not in a good way. Many wondered why he often wore a helmet in the field. (Michael Grossbardt)

Yankee catchers. He had played in nine World Series and would add a tenth when the Yankees traded him to Boston during the '67 season. (Maris added two more World Series with the Cardinals in 1967 and 1968.)

On opening day in 1967, Ellie's hit in the ninth inning off Red Sox rookie pitcher Bill Rohr broke up a no-hitter. Red Sox fans booed him for this all season when the Yankees played at Fenway Park. But now, not only was he traded to Boston, he helped them win their first pennant in twenty-one years. And in 1969, as he was promised, he returned to the Yankees to become the first African-American coach in American League history.

The end was arriving for Mantle as well. At thirty-six, he played his last game with the team as the 1968 season ended. His last two years were spent as a first baseman—his legs would no longer support him in covering the ground a center fielder had to cover. In spring training of 1969, without ever putting on the uniform, he announced his retirement.

This led to Mickey Mantle Day later that summer, a wonderful gathering of old teammates before a packed Yankee Stadium. Without notes, Mantle recalled Lou Gehrig's speech in which Lou said he was the "luckiest man on the face of the earth."

"Now I know how Lou Gehrig felt," he said.

His number 7 was retired, joining Ruth's 3, Gehrig's 4, and DiMaggio's 5. Later on, other numbers would be retired too, including Billy Martin (1), Derek Jeter (2), Joe Torre (6), Yogi Berra and Bill Dickey (both 8), Roger Maris (9), Phil Rizzuto (10), Thurman Munson (15), Whitey Ford (16), Don Mattingly (23), Elston Howard (32), Casey Stengel (37), Mariano Rivera (42), Reggie Jackson (44), and Ron Guidry (49). The Yankees had more numbers retired than any other team and more players in the Hall of Fame. They ran out of single-digit numbers, unless someone gets zero one day.

While Mantle was out, 1969 did see the debut of an exciting new player named Thurman Munson, who would make a place for himself in that line of great Yankee catchers that ran Dickey-Berra-Howard.

Munson was a catcher at Kent State University in Ohio and was named All-American catcher in 1968. He considered that a greater honor than winning the Rookie of the Year award in 1970, for he was up against hundreds of catchers for the college honor. In Rookie of the Year voting, he was competing with only a handful of qualified rookies.

Munson was the Yankees' top draft choice in 1968, and he played only ninety-nine games in the minor leagues before becoming the Yankees' regular catcher in 1970. And what a good one he was.

He was scrappy yet durable—he never went on the disabled list in his entire career. One year he made only one error all season, and that was when he was knocked unconscious in a hard collision play at the plate and dropped the ball.

Pitchers loved working with him because he knew each hitter's weaknesses, or would learn them in one game. He wasn't afraid of pitches in the dirt, and would even encourage pitchers to throw there if he thought it would force the batter into swinging at a bad pitch. He never feared passed balls or errors. He was tough as nails at his position and had a great throwing arm, although an injury some years later made him sometimes throw wildly in his hurry to grip the ball and fire.

At bat, he was a .300 hitter from the start. He did not hit a lot of home runs but showed power when he got the right pitch. He drove in a hundred runs three years in a row without hitting twenty homers in any of those seasons. This showed what a clutch hitter he was with men on base, and that he didn't have to hit it over the fence to deliver the runs. He was what was called a great "gap hitter," placing hard line drives between the outfielders.

Old-time players loved Munson because of how he played the game. It reminded them of their time, when you went all out for the team. Thurman knew that over the course of a long season, even good teams would lose sixty or more games a year. But he never took those losses well. He could be very grumpy after a loss.

Around the same time that Munson came up, the Boston Red Sox found a terrific catcher in Carlton Fisk. Fisk and Munson would get into a fight early in their careers over a bang-bang collision at home, and from that grew the rivalry between the two teams that continued for many, many years. Before Munson and Fisk, fans could walk up to the ticket window at Yankee Stadium or Fenway Park, buy a ticket, and sit there with a lot of empty seats around them. But by the early seventies, both teams started to get good at the same time, and the rivalry really grew. Eventually they would fight for first place almost every year. Red Sox fans became part of "Red Sox Nation." An owner of the Red Sox called the Yankees the "Evil Empire" when they kept going after the good free-agent players. It only added to the rivalry, which helped sell a lot of tickets and a lot of T-shirts, produced a lot of big television ratings, and made for a lot of memorable games.

CHAPTER 35

Building Back

With Roy White and Bobby Murcer in place, the arrival of Munson was an important building block toward the Yankees getting back into pennant contention. Mel Stottlemyre was still the leader of the pitching staff, but in 1972 the Yankees pulled off a good deal with the Red Sox late in spring training, bringing Sparky Lyle to New York.

Not many players had been traded between the Yankees and Red Sox over the years. Babe Ruth, of course, was the best known. Red Ruffing was a bad Red Sox pitcher who became a great Yankee pitcher. Lyle was the third of note to make the move.

Sparky, a fun-loving left-hander, had a big personality to go with a terrific hard slider. (If a fan sent a birthday cake to a Yankee and it was delivered to the clubhouse, Sparky would sit on it just to get a laugh out of his teammates.) The Yankees sent a first baseman, Danny Cater, to the Sox to get him. Lyle was a player they had long had their eyes on, a player who would be what is today called a closer, but back then was called a "short man" in the bull pen—a guy who pitched just an inning or two. Sometimes three.

Roy White is one of the best left fielders in Yankee history, and he was one from the Horace Clarke Era to still be around for the pennants of the '70s. (Michael Grossbardt)

Saves had only become a recorded baseball statistic in 1959, and many of them were recorded over two or three innings of work. The one-inning closer would not come along until the late 1980s. For now, a player like Lyle would be the model of a relief star. And he played the role well.

In his first season, when he had thirty-five saves, he finished third in Most Valuable Player voting. In those days, relief pitchers would enter games in golf carts or cars from the television sponsor. Sparky would come into home games in a pinstripe-painted Datsun (today the company is called Nissan), and the Yankee Stadium organist would play "Pomp and Circumstance," which many people think of as the graduation march at high school and college ceremonies. The music meant "the close, the end" because that was what his appearance usually meant. The fans would cheer as soon as they heard the first notes. Then Sparky would fling open the passenger door, toss his jacket to the waiting batboy, storm to the mound, fire his warm-ups, and take charge. It was a great show, and he immediately became a darling of Yankee fans.

He was fearless and daring. When Ringling Bros. Circus came to town, the promoters brought a tiger to Yankee Stadium for a game against the Detroit Tigers. Sparky let the tiger lick his face, and the photo was on the cover of the *Sporting News*. Not many people would do such a thing!

Sparky Lyle joined the team in 1972 and his "entrance music" created a new form of entertainment at ballparks. (Michael Grossbardt)

His control of the hard slider was awesome. Like Mariano Rivera's cutter years later, it was almost unhittable.

People seldom think about the red seams on a baseball, but it is those raised seams that allow pitchers to throw breaking balls—curves, sliders, cutters, splitters,

Bobby Murcer was promoted as a successor to Mickey Mantle (both were from Oklahoma) and he became a fan favorite from the time he arrived. (Michael Grossbardt)

forkballs, knuckleballs, and more. And that is what makes baseball baseball. If the ball did not have those seams, if it was like a billiard ball—smooth and perfect— it would not curve, and pitchers would only be able to throw straight pitches. It would be an entirely different game—a hitter's game for sure. Pitching would not count for much except for speed.

Lyle's big season of 1972 began to recharge Yankee fans. Murcer was a very popular player with a good Yankee Stadium swing that produced thirty-three home runs that year. White had speed and bat control. Even though he choked up on the bat, he was often the team's cleanup hitter. He was clutch—one year he set a record by driving in seventeen runs just with sacrifice flies.

The rest of the team seemed like a work in progress, but on Labor Day of 1972, with just four weeks left in the season, the Yankees were only one-half game out of first. It seemed like old days, and excitement was building. They were on the cover of *Sports Illustrated*! It had been a long time.

But the team collapsed in September and finished fourth. It was eight years in a row now without a pennant. A lot of new fans had come along and discovered baseball—usually around age six or seven—who had never known a Yankee championship season. And fans were losing patience with the manager, Ralph Houk, who had lost the glory of his first three years producing three pennants.

And there was another problem brewing at Yankee Stadium. It was Yankee Stadium itself. The year 1973 would be the fiftieth anniversary of the famous ballpark. But along the way, structural problems were developing. The concrete was weakening.

It was especially difficult on Bat Day, when young fans would bang their bats onto the ground to try to make noise and get a rally going. The banging caused more concrete to break apart, and it became a dangerous situation.

The Yankees, led by Michael Burke, met with New York City officials, led by Mayor John Lindsay, as early as 1971 to see what could be done. It was finally concluded that a major repair was needed, so 1973 would not only be the fiftieth anniversary, but it would also be the final year in the original "House That Ruth Built." Except for the outer walls, the ballpark would be rebuilt over a two-year period, and in the meantime, the Yankees would have to find another place to play.

CHAPTER 36

The Boss Arrives

The plans for a rebuilt stadium were all in place when a major announcement was made just after New Year's Day in 1973. The team was being sold by CBS to a group of investors headed by forty-two-year-old George M. Steinbrenner III, a shipbuilder from Cleveland.

Steinbrenner was a sportsman as well as a businessman. He had been an assistant college football coach and had owned a pro basketball team, although not in the NBA. He had tried to buy the Cleveland Indians, but without success. Now he heard that the Yankees might be for sale. He put a group of businessmen together, made Michael Burke a partner, and went with Burke to CBS prepared to pay ten million dollars for the team.

That was a steal. It was less than CBS had bought the team for nine years earlier, and the first time that the value of a major league team had ever gone down. No one else was bidding; no one knew it might be for sale. CBS was happy to get rid of the team, which had produced no winners during all the time they'd owned it.

And so George Steinbrenner entered baseball. He was not known to fans or to baseball people, but he began to make himself known quickly. He criticized the players whose hair was too long. He had little patience with players who didn't perform well. He promised the fans that within three years, he would give them a winner. He was a tough boss, and even a tough partner. Michael Burke left in a few months. A lot of front-office people resigned. Eventually newspapers took to calling him "the Boss." He would become the best-known owner in all of sports. And because he was a very active owner—involved in trades, never shy about being quoted in the news, not afraid to publicly criticize a player—he changed the way owners operated. Before him, owners were seldom heard from. It was almost always the general manager who was the "face" of the front office.

After Lee MacPhail resigned to become the president of the American League, the first of Steinbrenner's general managers was Gabe Paul, an old veteran of the game who had been in baseball since the 1930s. Paul, like Steinbrenner, was from Cleveland. He had run the Cleveland Indians for many years. He was the first in a very long line of general managers with the Yankees who came and went in the 1970s, 1980s, and 1990s, most of them finding frustration trying to make the Boss happy. It wasn't easy.

Graig Nettles, a terrific fielder, came to the Yankees from the Indians in 1973, and he was to become the team's regular third baseman over the next eleven years. He reminded a lot of people of Roger Maris—a great left-handed Yankee Stadium swing, number 9 on his back, and a similar personality. He would even become the first Yankee since Maris to lead the league in home runs.

The year 1973 also brought about a new rule in baseball: the designated hitter rule. The idea was to send a batter up to hit for the pitcher every time the pitcher was due, since pitchers were usually bad hitters. Although many had been the best hitters on their Little League teams, when they took pitching more seriously, they usually stopped practicing their hitting.

The American League took on the DH rule to get some more punch in their lineups—a DH instead of a pitcher. They had fallen behind the National League in run production and wanted to shake things up. It was supposed to be an

Graig Nettles won a home run title for the Yankees and played a brilliant third base. (Michael Grossbardt)

experiment, but it stuck. Only the National League refused to use it. Colleges, minor leagues, and baseball organizations in other nations all adopted it.

As it happened, the Yankees–Red Sox game on opening day in 1973 was the first in baseball that afternoon, and in the top of the first inning, Ron Blomberg got to be the first DH in a major league game. (He walked with the bases loaded in Fenway Park, getting an RBI.) Blomberg, who had been the team's first draft choice the year before Munson, was also the first Jewish Yankee in many years, and he wrote a book years later called *Designated Hebrew.*

The Yankees were playing well in 1973, looking like they had been in '72—and hoping they could go the distance this time. The Mets, meanwhile, were proving to be pesky competition. They had won the World Series in 1969, a "Miracle Mets" season, and aside from the Baltimore Orioles, who they'd beaten in the series, nobody felt it harder than the Yankees. And in 1973, not only were the Mets going to the World Series again, but they were now managed by Yogi Berra, who had become a Mets coach after the Yankees fired him in 1964.

The Yankees, though, were collapsing again. They stumbled back to fourth place. Fans were now booing Houk every time he came out of the dugout. Steinbrenner was losing patience with him too. He was from the "old ownership," and when new owners come along, changes usually follow.

On the final day of the season—the last game in the original Yankee Stadium—Houk resigned. He would go on to manage Detroit and later Boston, but his Yankee days were over. He had started with the Yankees as a minor league player in 1939, but it was now time to move on. (He owned a boat by his Florida home called *Thanks Yanks*).

As for the ballpark, there was a lot of disorder after the last game. Fans wanted souvenirs. People didn't think of "how much this is worth" as much then as they do now, but a lot of people scooped up dirt or yanked their seats out of the concrete and carted them home. Many of the remaining seats were sold by a discount department store for $5.75 each plus five cigarette proof-of-purchase coupons. A smart early collector named Bert Randolph Sugar paid the Yankees $1,500 to haul off all the treasures he could find in various storerooms in the Stadiums—old posters, signs, even contracts.

The morning after the last game, ceremonies were held on the field. Mrs. Babe Ruth was presented with home plate. Mrs. Lou Gehrig received first base.

There would have been a lot more sentiment had the team not fallen on such hard times. It was now nine years since a post-season appearance.

CHAPTER 37

Two Years at Shea

The Yankees would now move to Shea Stadium in Queens to share that park with the Mets over the next two seasons. It was like sharing the Polo Grounds with the Giants, which they had done many years before. It never felt right; the players thought it felt like a two-year road trip. They used the clubhouse normally used by the New York Jets football team.

The team's new manager was Bill Virdon, a longtime National League outfielder and manager who had long ago been a Yankees minor leaguer. He was not the first choice—their top pick was Dick Williams, who had won the World Series managing the Oakland Athletics. But the owner of the A's, Charlie Finley, would not let him go without receiving two players in return, and the Yankees turned to Virdon.

At Shea, the new faces on the team included outfielder Lou Piniella and first baseman Chris Chambliss. They would be the next building blocks.

Piniella had a great smile and an intense temper (which could go away in seconds), and he was always exciting to watch. His teammates loved to tease him, and he could give it right back. He was very popular and a very productive hitter, too.

Chambliss came from Cleveland at the end of April in 1974. The Yankees traded four pitchers to the Indians for him, including the veteran Fritz Peterson, who would surely have had a better record with a better infield and more hitting behind him all these years. In fact, he had the lowest home earned run average of any pitcher in Yankee Stadium history.

Chambliss, quiet, broad-shouldered, and strong, was the son of a navy chaplain, and was the Rookie of the Year in 1971, the year after Munson won it. He would now take over at first base and would usually hit cleanup in the lineup.

The Yankees were good guests at Shea, but one day, on Salute to the Army Day during a Yankees game, cannons were fired in the outfield as part of the pregame ceremonies. The cannon fire managed to knock down a portion of the fence in center field, and the start of the game had to be held up while it was temporarily repaired. So you could say the Yankees were good guests, except for the day they blew up the Shea Stadium fence.

Early on, Bill Virdon made a big defensive move with his outfield. As a one-time center fielder himself, he placed a high value on defense. The Yankees had obtained a fine defensive center fielder named Elliott Maddox over the winter, and Virdon decided to move Murcer to right and put Maddox in center.

Bobby wasn't happy. He was proud to play center—where DiMaggio and Mantle had been. But 1974 was an awful year for him. He didn't hit a home run in Shea until September. Maddox, however, did play a fine center field, and even hit .300. The Yankees were again in the pennant race, and this time, it looked like they might make it!

But with just the final weekend left, the team arrived very late at night at their hotel in Milwaukee. There had been some teasing going on, and at that hour, it wasn't taken well. A fight broke out in the lobby. Murcer, trying to be a peace-maker, injured his finger and would be unable to play. The Yankees went down in defeat, and the championship again got away from them. They had been close, but it was not to be.

Still, Virdon was named Manager of the Year by the *Sporting News*—but yet again, no pennant.

A few weeks after the season ended, general manager Gabe Paul pulled off a huge one-for-one deal with the San Francisco Giants. He traded Murcer, still the team's most popular player, for Bobby Bonds, one of the best players in the game. It was an enormous deal, one that shocked Murcer and saddened his fans. But in Bonds, who had power and speed, they had a huge talent. (Bobby was the father of Barry Bonds, who would become the all-time home run champion of baseball.)

Then another development came along.

Charles Finley, the owner of the Oakland Athletics, had been late making a payment to his pitcher Jim "Catfish" Hunter. Because the payment was part of

Catfish Hunter's New Year's Eve signing in 1974 was the first million-dollar baseball contract.
(Michael Grossbardt)

Hunter's contract, an arbiter ruled that Finley had voided the contract and that Hunter was a free agent, able to sign with anyone he wanted. He was cut loose from the reserve clause, that clause in baseball contracts that kept players tied to their teams forever, unless they were released or traded. Even if a player retired, and then decided to come back years later, his team still "owned" him.

With Hunter free, teams began to bid for him. The biggest contract in baseball at that point had been Hank Aaron's $200,000 with the Atlanta Braves. The Yankees had had three $100,000 players—DiMaggio, Mantle, and Murcer. Now teams were talking in the millions. And one by one, they all sent representatives to Hunter's farm in North Carolina to try to persuade him to play for them.

The Yankees had an edge. Their scout, Clyde Kluttz, was the same scout who had signed him to play for the Athletics years earlier. Now he worked for the Yankees, and Hunter liked him a lot. Kluttz still called Hunter "Jimmy"; "Catfish" had been invented by Finley, the owner of the A's, to give him a colorful nickname. People who really knew Hunter called him Jimmy.

Hunter was really worth a big contract. He was the Cy Young Award winner as best pitcher in the league. He had won twenty-one or more games four years in a row. He had great control, never missed a start, and was a real team leader. The A's had been to the World Series three years in a row with him.

Hunter's decision came on New Year's Eve, as 1974 was turning to 1975. He signed a five-year contract with the Yankees worth around three million dollars and flew to New York for a press conference that very night.

Baseball changed forever that night. Now players would regularly sign deals lasting more than a year, something that had rarely been done before. They would use sports agents to negotiate the best possible deals for them. And they would make big money if a free agent system could ever be established for everyone. For now, the deal benefitted only Hunter, and only because Finley was late with a payment.

So the Yankees went into 1975 having just missed in '74, with Bonds and Hunter now on their roster. At last they were favored to win the pennant after ten years.

But they didn't. In fact, they didn't come close. Hunter pitched great, won

Billy Martin was named Yankees manager five times—and was fired five times.
(Michael Grossbardt)

twenty-three games, and threw thirty complete games, something that would be unthinkable today. Bonds played hard but suffered some injuries that took away some of his high-achieving game. But the team just couldn't put it all together.

Nobody was more disappointed than Steinbrenner. He had tried to produce a winner, had paid a lot of money for Hunter, and now the team was underperforming. Steinbrenner was about to make another dramatic move.

In Texas, Billy Martin was fired as manager of the Rangers. It had been eighteen years since the Yankees had traded him. The owners who did that were long gone. Since then he had become a respected manager, leading Minnesota, Detroit, and Texas to strong seasons. He still had his problems with fights and with drinking, but no one questioned his abilities in the dugout while the game was on.

In buying the Yankees, Steinbrenner had purchased not only the active team but the team's history. He loved "owning" Ruth, Gehrig, DiMaggio, Berra, Ford, and Mantle. He didn't *really* own them, but by owning the Yankees he could embrace their part of the team's great lore. And to him, Billy Martin represented the winning ways of the great Yankees of the past. He wanted Billy.

Virdon was fired and Martin was hired right on Old-Timers' Day in 1975. Billy nearly cried when he put on his old number 1 uniform. The fans were thrilled, although younger ones didn't remember Billy as a player. But after so many losing years, it just felt like this change would be for the best.

"Wait till I have the team for a whole spring training," he said. "Watch what we can do."

That meant wait for 1976, and that seemed fine, because great excitement was building for that year. It would be a return to Yankee Stadium—the new Yankee Stadium, all modern, with escalators, with no poles blocking views, with a great new scoreboard and with a fresh outlook.

The Yankees also sprang more trades over the winter in an effort to give Martin a team that could win it all. From the Angels, for Bonds, they got center fielder Mickey Rivers, who would be a speedy leadoff hitter and steal a lot of bases, and pitcher Ed Figueroa, a Puerto Rican–born pitcher. From the Pirates they got twenty-one-year-old second baseman Willie Randolph, who came from Brooklyn, and veteran pitcher Dock Ellis, who would join the starting rotation.

Randolph, who made the All-Star team in his rookie season, was perhaps the most welcome. After years of Horace Clarke and then a short period with Sandy Alomar Sr., the fans were happy to have someone so young with all this promise. These were still the days when middle infielders—second basemen and shortstops—weren't expected to hit that much. It was defense that was important, and Randolph gave it to them.

Good times were coming.

CHAPTER 38

Returning Home to Glory Days

Before the '76 season began, Martin asked Munson to serve as team captain. It had been Steinbrenner's idea. The Yankees had not had a captain since Lou Gehrig died in 1941. Joe McCarthy had retired the position with Gehrig.

Reminded of this, Steinbrenner said, "If Joe McCarthy knew Thurman Munson, he'd know this was the right guy."

Thurman had always led by example. He would continue to do so, but now he was the Yankees' first captain in more than thirty-five years. Not DiMaggio, not Dickey, not Berra, not Mantle—none of them had had the job.

Thurman Munson would win the Most Valuable Player award in 1976, his first year as captain.

Speaking of Berra, Yogi was back. Fired as manager of the Mets, he had "come home" for 1976, joining Martin's coaching staff. That could only be seen as good luck. Maybe the curse was lifted—they hadn't won since he was fired as Yankees manager.

The season began with a funny game in Milwaukee. Martin called on a

Four great Yankee catchers shown at Old-Timers' Day in 1976—(left to right) Bill Dickey, Yogi Berra, Elston Howard, Thurman Munson. (Michael Grossbardt)

young reliever named Dave Pagan to pitch the ninth inning in relief of Lyle. The Brewers were losing 9–6, and the bases were loaded.

Pagan was pale and skinny and nervous-looking. He came from a town in Canada that was so small, his telephone number was 8. Just 8.

He promptly gave up a grand slam home run to the Brewers' Don Money to give Milwaukee a shocking victory. But wait! Chambliss at first had called time. Immediately Martin ran out on the field to argue that the pitch did not count.

Pagan only saw Martin running out, looking furious. He thought the manager was coming out to beat him up for allowing the home run!

But no, he was out to argue—and he won the argument. Time had been called. Given a second chance, Pagan got Money on a fly to right, and the Yankees went on to win the game. It was a close call for everyone, but a good sign for the new season.

In fact, the new season was a hit. The new Yankee Stadium opened with old Bob Shawkey throwing out the first pitch. He had been the opening-game pitcher when the original stadium opened in 1923! Many greats were on hand, included Mrs. Ruth, Mrs. Gehrig, DiMaggio, Mantle, and of course Berra. The Yankees were always terrific at ceremonies and at bringing old stars together for special events.

They lost that opening game, but the rest of the season unfolded as though they were the Yankees of old. There wasn't much suspense. Billy Martin did as promised—he had a team that he put together in spring training, and he took them all the way to win the American League East with ease.

Division play had begun in 1969. Before that, if you won the pennant, you went to the World Series. This was the first time the Yankees were ever in the postseason where they first had to defeat a league opponent before going to the Series.

The opponent was the Kansas City Royals. And they fought the Yankees tough, with the final game of the five-game series going down to the ninth inning. Chris Chambliss was the leadoff hitter against the Royals' reliever Mark Littell.

Chris had hit a home run in July to win a game, and the fans wouldn't leave until he came out of the dugout to wave and acknowledge their cheers. The term "walk-off home run" didn't exist yet, and this waving to the crowd was thought to be the first time that had been done since Roger Maris hit his sixty-first home run fifteen years before.

Chambliss now swung at Littell's first pitch and hit it high into the night. It landed over the wall for a game-winning, pennant-winning home run. The fans raced onto the field, and Chambliss had to run like a football running back to get around the bases, knocking people aside as he did. He never did get near home plate, but raced for his life toward the dugout. The fans had mobbed the field, and it would be a long time before they went home.

And when they did, Chambliss went to home plate and touched it. Or touched where it was supposed to be. Someone had taken home plate home.

And so after twelve years, the Yankees were back to the World Series! For Roy White, who had been there since 1965, it was extra sweet. The proud switch-hitter from Compton, California, was going to get a ring at last.

Unfortunately for the Yankees, they were tired, their pitching rotation was not positioned for this new series, and they were facing one of the great teams of all time, the Cincinnati Reds and their "Big Red Machine" of Johnny Bench, Pete Rose, Joe Morgan, Tony Perez, and others. The Reds pounded them, winning in four straight and taking a lot of the joy out of the Chambliss homer and the pennant season. It was a tough way to go down after such a great season.

Steinbrenner had everyone at work the next day. It was time to do whatever it took to get to the next level and win a world championship. The pennant was nice, but Steinbrenner wanted the Yankees to be about World Series victories. He painted the years of those championships on the walls in Yankee Stadium, but left out the ones that were "only" pennants.

It was to be all—or nothing.

Chris Chambliss sent the Yankees to their first World Series in twelve years with a walk-off home run against Kansas City in 1976. (Michael Grossbardt)

CHAPTER 39

Reggie and the Bronx Zoo

There was now a new rule in place to help teams improve.

Free agency had come to baseball.

After the Catfish Hunter decision, baseball players, led by their union leader Marvin Miller, had won another arbitration decision. This one led to the creation of a free agent system, under which players could, after six years in the majors, declare themselves to be free agents and sign somewhere else—of their choosing.

The first free agent class included one of Cincinnati's best pitchers, Don Gullett, and the Yankees signed him. But they also had their eyes on the biggest star available, the powerful outfielder Reggie Jackson.

Jackson had been Hunter's teammate in Oakland and was one of the brightest stars in baseball. Nobody left the room when Reggie was at bat. Like Babe Ruth, he could excite you with a home run, and he could excite you with a big strikeout. (He had the most strikeouts in baseball history.)

"If I ever played in New York," he said, "they would name a candy bar after me." (He was thinking of the Baby Ruth candy bar, which the manufacturer claimed was not named for Babe Ruth. They didn't want to have to pay Babe Ruth to use his name. Also, Yogi Berra was never paid for the cartoon character Yogi Bear, who was obviously named for him.)

Many teams went after Reggie. Steinbrenner made him a personal project, walking with him on the streets of Manhattan to feel the city's energy and excitement, to hear people yell, "Hey, Reggie, you gotta sign with the Yankees!"

He got him. Jackson signed a five-year contract to play for the Yankees, took uniform number 44 (he liked the way it looked on Hank Aaron), and got ready to bring his own excitement to New York. He got just under three million dollars, along with a new Rolls-Royce.

And not long afterward, a candy bar was named for him. The Reggie bar. And he got paid for that, too.

Missing from the press conference where the Yankees signed Jackson was Billy Martin. Martin was not happy. He did not want a big personality like Reggie on the team, and he did not want the Boss filling out his roster. Although Reggie was a natural cleanup hitter, Martin refused to bat him there for most of the season. The two of them came to dislike each other.

Reggie added to the problem when he did an interview with a national magazine and questioned whether Munson was a "true captain." He told the reporter, "I'm the straw that stirs the drink. Munson can only stir it bad." (Reggie later denied saying this.)

Munson was extremely popular not only with fans but with his teammates, yet when the story was published early in the 1977 season, the Yankee players supported Thurman and kept their distance from Jackson. Jackson felt unaccepted and was not going to tone down his large ego and outspoken ways to fit in. It made for a very awkward situation in the clubhouse. There were times when it felt like the only solution was to trade Reggie, despite it being his first season. That certainly would have made Martin happy.

Day in and day out, things were said in the newspapers by Martin, by Munson, by Jackson, by Steinbrenner, and by Gabe Paul, the general manager. It created such a stressful clubhouse that it would come to be known as "the Bronx Zoo."

On June 18 things really turned bad—and on national television. The Yankees were playing the Red Sox in Fenway Park when it appeared that Reggie loafed on a fly ball to right that dropped in front of him for a hit.

Martin was furious. This was one thing that professionals did not do. And so right there, with the Yankees in the field, he sent Paul Blair to right with instructions to tell Reggie to return to the dugout—he was through for the day.

This was another thing professionals did not do: show up a player in front of everyone.

Reggie got to the dugout, and Martin's temper exploded. If the team's coaches (including Howard and Berra) did not hold them apart, it seemed clear that they would have starting swinging at each other with the TV cameras rolling.

It was an embarrassment all around. And most of the hard-working sportswriters who tried to keep up with these breaking news stories thought that Steinbrenner was going to fire Martin.

But it didn't happen. Cooler heads talked him out of it. But Reggie was in a very bad situation. His manager and most of the team thought little of him. And this was just the first year of a five-year contract!

This was such high drama that in years to come, there would be books about this era, an ESPN miniseries, and even a Broadway show.

Meanwhile, the team was winning and drawing big crowds. The controversy was making the Yankees big news in New York. A new young pitcher, Ron Guidry, was exciting the crowds in his first full season, winning sixteen games after almost quitting baseball the year before. He'd been sent back to the minor leagues for more seasoning, after having been with the Yankees for several years. Frustrated, he decided to quit and was driving home to Louisiana when his wife convinced him to turn around and keep trying to get back on the major league team. And he made it. He didn't give up.

The team also had a new shortstop. His name was Bucky Dent, and he came over in a trade with the White Sox. Bucky was very handsome—he even starred

Ron "the Gator" Guidry had an amazing 25–3 record in 1978, and fans stood after he got two strikes on batters, setting a new Yankee Stadium standard. (Michael Grossbardt)

in a movie—and female fans bought his posters and started going to games to cheer for him. Where once a crowd at Yankee Stadium had very few females in the stands, now there were many female fans. And Bucky Dent's good looks had a lot to do with it!

A Yankee veteran by this point—Sparky Lyle—was so good out of the bull pen that he would become the first relief pitcher in American League history to win the Cy Young Award as the league's top pitcher. And his work was good enough to help the Yankees win a hundred games and a second straight division title.

Again they faced Kansas City in the American League Championship Series, and again they won, even though Martin benched the slumping Reggie in the deciding fifth game. All those millions for a big bat at cleanup, and yet Reggie was on the bench.

But nine days later, bringing to a close one of the most tension-filled seasons the team had ever played, Reggie rose to the occasion and hit three home runs on three pitches in the deciding game of the World Series against the Los Angeles Dodgers. He had five in the Series—a record—but the three-in-one game on a cold October night at Yankee Stadium made baseball history. The crowd went crazy as Reggie came out of the dugout to wave and thank them for their cheers. He had become, with those swings, "Mr. October." It would one day be on his Hall of Fame plaque. Even Martin and Munson were smiling in the dugout—the big guy had come through. He had been the difference, after all, between losing the 1976 series to Cincinnati and winning the '77 series against the Dodgers.

The Yankees had their first world championship in fifteen years. They would have their first-ever ticker-tape parade up Broadway.

The Yanks were back on top!

Although only a Yankee for five seasons, Reggie Jackson was a memorable one. (Michael Grossbardt)

CHAPTER 40

The Bucky Dent Game

The free agency system was only a year old when the Yankees made another big signing, getting Rich "Goose" Gossage after the '77 season. Gossage was a twenty-six-year-old relief star who threw very hard with a very intimidating style—a lot of big winding motion from his arms and his legs.

Many questioned the signing, because Sparky Lyle was already a star relief pitcher and had just won the Cy Young Award. He was just as imposing on the mound as Gossage. The main difference was that Gossage was seven years younger.

"Sparky went from Cy Young to sayonara," said Graig Nettles, using the Japanese word for "good-bye."

Lyle was obviously not happy about this, and unfortunately for him during the 1978 season, Gossage got most of the save opportunities—and did great. After the season, Sparky would be traded to Texas, and he went on to write a book called *The Bronx Zoo*, which told a lot of funny stories—and some tension-filled ones—about the season. It was a bestseller.

The Gossage signing said a lot about the Yankees' future. If they could get a star player a lot younger than the one they had, they would go for it. Just like when they'd traded old Hank Bauer for young Roger Maris, or replaced old Tony Lazzeri with young Joe Gordon. And if they could trade some minor leaguers for a proven major league player, they would go for that, too. No matter how promising the minor league players were, there was always the question of whether they could play in the big leagues—let alone on the big stage of Yankee Stadium. It was much safer to get an established player and reduce the risk, assuming they could afford the established player's higher salary.

And they could.

On opening day of the 1978 season, Reggie Jackson homered his first time up, and the fans—who all got free Reggie bars as a promotion—threw the bars onto the field in happiness. It was great promotion for the candy bar, because everyone wrote about it.

Despite Reggie's homer, the season did not start well for the Yankees or for Gossage, and they were struggling to finish first. It looked like the Boston Red Sox were going to run away with the division. The best thing the Yankees had going for them was Ron "the Gator" Guidry, who was having one of the best seasons in baseball history, and Ed Figueroa, who was on his way to becoming the first Puerto Rican–born player to win twenty games in a season.

Otherwise, the team was struggling, and guess what? Jackson and Martin were feuding again.

On July 17, Martin ordered Jackson to bunt. Reggie had not done that in six years. Big power hitters hardly ever bunted anymore.

After one pitch, Martin removed the bunt sign, but Reggie, now angry and defiant, continued to attempt to bunt, eventually popping out. After the game, Martin suspended Jackson.

The suspension was lifted six days later. The team had won all their games while Reggie was away. Jackson denied that his act was "defiance."

Billy's anger soared. He was not happy about having Jackson back at all. He'd never wanted him in the first place. At the airport in Chicago, about to fly with the team to Kansas City, Billy told reporters that Jackson and Steinbrenner "deserve each other."

He then added, "One's a born liar; the other's convicted."

Oh boy. He had just called his boss a convicted liar. George Steinbrenner had been suspended from baseball in 1973 when he was convicted of illegal campaign contributions through his employees to President Richard Nixon's reelection fund, and for making his employees lie about them. So Billy had really hit a sore point with this one.

Billy was gone. Fired. The only job he ever really wanted was to manage the Yankees, and now it was over, less than two years after he was hired.

The team and the season were melting away. But then Steinbrenner did a very smart thing, and he also got lucky.

He had his new team president, Al Rosen, reach out and hire Bob Lemon to replace Martin. Lemon, a star pitcher and an old teammate of Rosen's with Cleveland, had recently been let go as manager of the White Sox. He was a perfect choice to calm the rough seas and restore order to the team. Everybody in baseball admired "Lem."

As for luck, the New York City newspapers soon went on strike, and there were no screaming headlines every day about the mess in the Yankee organization. Together with Lem's calm presence, things settled down.

Oh, there was still more drama. Steinbrenner had second thoughts about letting Martin go, and the fans missed the feisty little guy. So on Old-Timers' Day, just five days after he was fired, the Yankees snuck Martin into the stadium and took everyone by surprise by introducing him on the field and announcing that two years later—1980—he would return to again manage, with Lemon to become the general manager. Even Lemon wasn't told about this in advance.

Yes, it really was the Bronx Zoo.

But the team started to play better.

The Yanks arrived in Boston on September 7, just four games behind the Red Sox, and they proceeded to win all four games. The scores were 15–3, 13–2, 7–0,

Bucky Dent's home run against Boston in the 1978 tie-breaker game at Fenway Park earned him a place in Yankee history. (Michael Grossbardt)

and 7–4, and the newspapers (at least in Boston), called it the Boston Massacre.

At the end of the season, the Yankees and the Red Sox were tied for first. A play-off game had to be played, and the Red Sox won the coin toss. It would be in Fenway Park on Monday, October 2, the day after the regular season was supposed to have ended. It was the first tie-breaker game in the American League in thirty-two years. Guidry, who was 24–3 at this point, pitched against Boston's Mike Torrez, who had been a Yankee the year before. It was a sunny afternoon, and the place was packed for baseball history. A glorious day for baseball.

The Red Sox led 2–0 through six, and in the top of the seventh the Yankees got two men on and their ninth-place hitter, Bucky Dent, was at bat. A home run would put the Yankees ahead, but Bucky had hit only four home runs all season, and only twenty-two in his whole career.

Dent fouled a pitch off his foot and dropped in pain. His bat had cracked on the pitch, so he borrowed a bat from the on-deck hitter, Mickey Rivers. He returned to the batter's box and on the next pitch hit one over the Green Monster—the high green wall in left field—and the Yankees led 3–2! It was a miracle home run, and had the Yankees lost the coin toss, and had the game been in Yankee Stadium, it probably would not have gone out.

The Yanks got extra help on a home run by Jackson and won the game 5–4. Guidry, known as "Louisiana Lightning," finished 25–3 with a 1.74 ERA. He pitched nine shutouts and won the Cy Young Award with one of the greatest seasons of the twentieth century.

The Yanks proceeded to beat Kansas City in the American League Championship Series for the third year in a row, and then, for the second year in a row they beat the Dodgers in the World Series for another world championship. The team that had been fourteen games out of first in mid-July had come back all the way to defend their title. "Greatest Comeback Ever," it said on their World Series rings. For everyone who had to go through it, 1978 was exciting, dramatic, and emotionally draining. But they did it! And they would not win another World Series for eighteen years. It was almost as though the season took everything out of them.

CHAPTER 41

Season of Tragedy

In 1979 the Yankees weren't playing well. Catfish Hunter, in his final season, won only two games, but his overall impact on the team was monumental. He more than anyone had given the Yankees the sense that they were winners. He brought that with him from Oakland and went to the World Series three times in his five Yankee seasons. He retired as a beloved Yankee for the ages.

Meanwhile, Bob Lemon had been hailed as just the right man to manage the Yankees through that turbulent season, but ten days after the World Series ended, his son was killed in a car crash in Arizona. It was the worst thing that could happen to a parent, and right from the start of 1979, it seemed obvious that his heart was not in the job.

On June 18, Steinbrenner made the difficult decision to fire Bob Lemon and bring Billy Martin back a year earlier than planned. The team was barely above .500 and did not look like they were going to repeat as champions.

On June 26, they brought Bobby Murcer back to the Yankees. He came over from the Cubs and would stay with the team until 1983, mostly as a DH and pinch hitter, and as popular as ever. He would also reunite with his pal Thurman

Munson, two old teammates who had always kept in touch even while in different leagues, even if seldom seeing each other in person.

Munson by now was a pilot. He owned his own jet plane. He had begun to learn to fly the year before, purchasing a propeller-driven plane and flying home to his family in Ohio after games instead of driving home to a rented suburban home like most of the players did.

Munson had grown up in a difficult home in Canton, Ohio. His father, a truck driver, was absent much of the time, and when he was home, showed little affection for the four Munson children. He was hard to please. It was not a happy childhood.

When Thurman grew up and became a professional baseball player, he married his high school girlfriend, Diana, and they had three children. The youngest one, his son Michael, was somewhat hyperactive and needed his father around. Thurman remembered what his own childhood was like with that absent father, so he wanted to be able to go home as often as possible. That's why he learned to fly. He could be home in a couple of hours from Yankee Stadium. It was a good situation for him, and he became a terrific dad and a great family man. He was determined not to repeat what his own childhood had been like.

Players were now making big salaries (although not yet millions), and so he could afford the plane. And being the self-confident star player that he was, he quickly mastered the propeller plane and moved up to a jet. It would get him home even faster.

The Yankees finished a series in Chicago on August 1, 1979, and with a day off on the second, a Thursday, Munson flew his jet from Chicago to Canton, where he lived. He didn't have to be back to Yankee Stadium until Friday afternoon.

He took care of some business in the morning—he was buying a lot of real estate in the area—and had lunch with Diana's father, who he considered his best friend. Then he went to the airport where he kept the jet, bumped into two people he knew, and offered to take them up for a spin. He had only owned the new jet for three weeks. He had flown some teammates in it—including Reggie Jackson, with whom he had made peace.

Showing off the jet for the two friends he'd run into, Munson made a few "touch-and-go" landings, in which he would go up, circle around, land, and take off again to do it all over. He did this successfully three times.

On the fourth try, things went wrong. He was too low and coming in too fast for a landing. He wasn't wearing his seat belt. And he crashed.

The jet landed hard in a field next to the runway. All three survived the impact, but as the plane moved at high speed along the field, a wing crashed into a tree stump and brought the plane to a sudden halt. The two passengers tried to get Thurman out, but by not wearing a seat belt, the impact had jarred his body and left him paralyzed, unable to assist with his own rescue.

Suddenly the wreckage caught fire. The two passengers had to make the very tough decision to run for their lives, unable to free Thurman.

And Thurman died.

He was only thirty-two. The captain of the Yankees was gone.

The news shocked everyone. George Steinbrenner was in tears as he phoned his players one by one. The fans were stunned.

The next night, before a game against Baltimore, a moment of silence turned into a long, sad tribute to their fallen leader, as the players stood outside their dugouts and the fans yelled "Thur-man, Thur-man, Thur-man" and wiped away tears mixed with falling raindrops. It was immediately announced that no one would ever wear Thurman's number 15 again. The Yankees were at their positions on the field—but the catcher's position was left empty. Finally the memorial ended, a rookie catcher came out to catch, and the game went on.

Three days later the team went to Canton for Thurman's funeral. It was one of the saddest days in Yankee history, made even more so by the sight of Thurman's three small children, with his son Michael wearing a little number 15 Yankee uniform. Murcer and Piniella delivered eulogies for their beloved friend. Even the commissioner of baseball attended.

They still had a game to play that night, again in New York against the Orioles. Billy Martin told Murcer, "You go home—don't worry about the game. You've just lost your close friend and delivered a eulogy for him. It's enough for any man."

But Murcer told Martin, "Skip, I just feel like I need to play tonight, if that's okay with you."

And so Bobby played, and the Yankees were just going through the motions, not very happy to have a game on this night. But in the seventh inning, trailing 4–0, Murcer hit his first home run since returning to the Yankees. It was an emotional moment, and it lifted the whole team—got them focused again.

In the ninth, still trailing 4–3, Murcer was due to bat again, this time against a tough left-hander and former Yankee, Tippy Martinez.

Tippy had loved Munson when he was with the Yankees, and he suddenly remembered a time that Munson had come to the mound and told him to let Ron LeFlore—a Detroit hitter with a thirty-game hitting streak on the line—have a pitch he could hit. Not a batting-practice pitch, but a straight fastball that might give him a chance to at least make contact.

In an instant, Tippy remembered that. With runners on second and third, he had gotten two quick strikes on Murcer and felt that one more curve would strike him out.

But remembering the Ron LeFlore moment, he threw Bobby a straight fastball, a pitch he could handle. And Bobby lined it down the left-field line for a base hit. The tying run scored and the winning run scored! Tippy Martinez, walking off the field in defeat, looked up at the sky and said to himself, "That one was for you, Thurm."

Everyone was crying, deep in emotion. The whole five days—from the time of the crash to the moment of Murcer's winning hit—was like a Hollywood movie.

The season ended with the Yankees out of the play-offs. Then Billy Martin got into a barroom fight and was fired again for his generally bad behavior.

"We just can't keep having this kind of thing happen every two months," said Steinbrenner.

It was true. When Billy drank too much, he would go looking for a fight. Anyone who said the slightest thing to set him off was in for trouble. He was like an old Western gunslinger, looking for trouble. (He even owned a Western-wear clothing store in New York.)

Today people have come to recognize that alcoholism is an illness and there are treatments available. But during Billy Martin's time, few people thought like that, and he might have resisted treatment even if it was offered to him.

Even though he'd been fired, it was not the last time Yankee fans would hear from Billy Martin.

CHAPTER 42

Enter Dave Winfield

Billy's replacement was Dick Howser, who had been the team's third-base coach for ten years. With Howser's announcement as manager, the team also announced that Gene Michael would be the general manager. The two former infielders were both smart baseball people—Howser would later win a World Series managing Kansas City, and Michael would become much admired in the 1990s for his work bringing the Yankees back to glory. But now they were both rookies at their jobs, with a very demanding boss.

Helped by Tommy John winning twenty-two games (arm repair surgery, named for him, was first done on him in 1974), and forty-one home runs from Jackson, the Yankees won the division in 1980 but lost the League Championship Series in three straight to the Royals. Steinbrenner was beside himself over this "embarrassment" and fired Howser after just one year. His replacement was Michael, moving down from the general manager position. It was the start of a crazy stretch in which it was hard to remember who was managing and who was the general manager from year to year.

The next year, 1981, brought Dave Winfield to the Yankees, armed with a huge ten-year free agent contract. This would be the only season in which Winfield was teammates with Reggie Jackson, who would leave via free agency for the Angels after the season, his whole Yankee career just covering the five years of his original contract.

Winfield starred in baseball, football, and basketball in college, was drafted in all three sports, and converted from pitching to the outfield as a baseball player. He was six foot six and 220 pounds, and he spent eight productive seasons with San Diego. He had power, speed, and a great arm, and he was one of the most athletic players baseball had ever seen. He had established a foundation to help young people, and part of his new Yankee contract called for contributions by the team to that foundation.

When it was realized that there had been a misunderstanding over the amount of money his contract might ultimately cost the Yankees, it was pretty close to war between him and Steinbrenner, even after the contract was signed. Was it thirteen million dollars over ten years or was it twenty-five million? It wasn't exactly a small difference. The disagreement made for a very difficult relationship between the Boss and his star employee, which was never really resolved. Years of lawsuits between them would mark Winfield's time with the Yankees, during which he made it to the postseason only once—that very first year.

That first year was not a happy one for baseball. Although there had been a short strike by players at the start of the 1972 season, in 1981 they had a big one. For two months during the summer, the game was shut down as negotiators argued over the system of free agents. For a while, it looked like the season might not resume, but on August 10 it did, with about a third of the season lost.

The Yankees were in first place when the strike hit, but when play resumed, it was decided that the season would be a split season, with a first-half and a second-half winner, and an extra round of play-offs between those two winners.

By the time the Yankees were ready for the play-offs, Steinbrenner had fired Michael and brought back Bob Lemon to manage. Michael had been complaining about interference by the owner and almost forced Steinbrenner to fire him.

George Steinbrenner (center) with two of his many managers—Lou Piniella (left) and Gene Michael (right), both former Yankee players. (Michael Grossbardt)

He did.

The Yankees won the special play-off round against Milwaukee, and then knocked off Oakland (now managed by Billy Martin) in the League Championship Series. So although Michael had been the manager in the first half—which was the half that got the Yankees into the postseason—it would be Lemon managing in the World Series.

Yes, it was a strange season.

The World Series was again against the Dodgers, the only World Series in which Jackson and Winfield were teammates. Disappointingly, Winfield had only one single in six games, batting .045, and Steinbrenner sarcastically called him "Mr. May" to reporters, comparing him to "Mr. October."

The whole World Series was odd. Steinbrenner broke his thumb in what he said was a fight in a hotel elevator with fans who said bad things about the Yankees. And when the Series was over, and the Dodgers had won, Steinbrenner prepared a press release containing a written apology to Yankee fans for the "performance of the Yankee team."

Steinbrenner's apology did not make the players very happy. They had played their best but had been beaten by a team that was better than they were that week.

That's baseball. It happens.

CHAPTER 43

Tough Times in the Eighties

And so with Reggie Jackson gone, 1982 began a long run of finishing out of the play-offs. The difference between this period and the 1965–1975 gap was that these teams in the eighties had good players and actually won more regular-season games than any other team in that decade. But they always fell short, usually with a new manager, a new pitching coach, a new general manager, and free agents that often turned out to be disappointments.

In 1982 alone there were three managers. Lemon was fired again after only fourteen games, and Michael was brought back from scouting to replace him. Then Michael was fired again, and another scout, Clyde King, replaced him.

Guess who replaced King in 1983?

Billy Martin. It was Billy's third time on the job. Yes, Oakland had fired him, so he was available.

The eighties would mostly be marked by odd moments amid the comings and goings of promising players and hopeful managers.

There was, for example, the day Dave Winfield, warming up in the Toronto outfield between innings, playfully threw a ball at a seagull and accidentally killed it. Seagulls appeared each day in the Toronto outfield, just sitting there while the game went on. Winfield never expected the outcome with his throw, but Toronto police arrested him after the game on an animal rights violation. He was cleared.

The Yankees tried a fuzzy mascot in 1983 named Dandy. Having a mascot didn't seem like the sort of thing the Yankees did. Dandy didn't last long and isn't well remembered. It was said that Dandy was beaten senseless by some fans in the upper deck one evening. That may not have really happened, but after 1983, the Yankees decided not to use the mascot anymore.

There was the hot July Fourth day in 1983—George Steinbrenner's birthday—when Dave Righetti pitched a no-hitter in Yankee Stadium against the Red Sox.

"Rags" had come to the Yankees in the Sparky Lyle trade with Texas and would go from being a no-hit starting pitcher to one of the best relief pitchers in baseball. He had been Rookie of the Year in 1981, despite making only fifteen appearances as a starter, and the no-hitter was a big moment for him. But the very next year, 1984, he moved to the bull pen, and even set a major league record with forty-six saves in 1986.

The year 1983 saw the arrival of Don Mattingly with the Yankees. Only five-eleven and 185 pounds, he did not look as imposing as he turned out to be. He had a tight, compact swing, close to the body, and he drove the ball hard. He found a stroke perfect for Yankee Stadium and became the most popular player on the team, one of the great fan favorites in Yankee history. "Donnie Baseball," they called him, because he seemed to just "live the game," and worked so hard at it. A lot of fans had posters of him on their walls. In 1984, his first full year as a regular, he staged a terrific battle for the league's batting championship, beating out his teammate Dave Winfield .343 to .340 on the final day of the season. As they walked off the field, the fans cheered them both, but you could tell they were pulling for the little guy, the new hero in town.

Mattingly would have some magical moments besides that. He won the Most Valuable Player award in 1985. In 1986 he set a team record with 238 hits, and another with fifty-three doubles. He was also a fabulous first baseman, winning nine Gold Gloves at the position.

In 1987 he hit six grand slam home runs—a record for one season—and amazingly, they were the only six grand slams of his career. All in one year, plus another one in spring training, to boot! And that same year, he homered in eight consecutive games, yet another record.

But in '87 he started to develop back problems, and eventually the bad back

Don Mattingly (left) and Dave Winfield excited fans throughout the 1980s and battled for the league batting championship in 1984. (Rogers Photo Archives)

took away his power. The last six years of his career were not as good as the first six, and after it looked like he would be a Hall of Famer for sure, he fell short. But his popularity with the fans never faded—people just kept pulling for him to recover. It didn't happen.

To make it to the Hall of Fame, it is better for the second half of your career to be better than the first. Sandy Koufax and Kirby Puckett, from the Minnesota

Twins, are two good examples. If your best years are the first half, you don't have as good a chance.

Like Mattingly, Winfield was a force on the team and always one of the best players in the league, but he, too, had the bad fortune of being there when the team did not go to the postseason, other than his first year. In 1989 Dave had back surgery and missed the whole season. That was pretty much the end of his Yankee career, as he was traded early in 1990, ending his run with the team.

On July 24, 1983, one of the strangest plays in baseball history happened at Yankee Stadium.

The Kansas City Royals' great star George Brett hit a two-run home run in the ninth inning off Gossage. It put the Royals ahead and silenced the crowd.

But Graig Nettles, by now the team captain, told Billy Martin that Brett's bat had too much sticky pine tar on it—the rule said pine tar couldn't go more than halfway up the bat.

Martin came out and argued, and the umpire, Tim McClelland, measured the bat to see if Martin was right.

He was. McClelland raised his thumb and called Brett out for using an illegal bat.

Brett burst out of the dugout screaming and yelling, his rage growing by the second. It looked like he was ready to take on the whole world. Two runs came off the scoreboard, and the Yankees held on to win 4–3.

But wait!

The Royals appealed the call, and league president Lee MacPhail (the former Yankees general manager), ruled that the home run counted! He said that even though the umpire's call was correct, the rule was wrong. Pine tar really didn't make a difference that should cost the man his home run.

This, of course, infuriated the Yankees, especially Martin and Steinbrenner. The Royals were ordered to return to New York almost a month later to finish the game, starting from where Brett had homered. Of course, he had been thrown out of the game by then for arguing. He stayed at the airport while the team went to the stadium to play the final outs of the game. Martin refused to take it seriously, even though he should have. He played Mattingly, a left-hander, at second base and Guidry in center field. The Yankees went down 1-2-3 in their half of the ninth and lost the game. It would forever be known as "the Pine Tar Game."

CHAPTER 44

Yogi, Once More

Billy Martin had his usual list of bad behavior moments in 1983 and was fired again after the season. This time he was replaced by his coach, Yogi Berra—twenty years after Yogi had been fired after winning the 1964 pennant. He had been a Yankees coach since returning from the Mets in 1976.

Everyone loved Yogi, and this time around he would actually get to manage his son Dale, who had been traded to the Yankees by Pittsburgh.

Mattingly gave Yogi a lot of credit for moving him to first base from the outfield, full-time. But it was a tough season for Berra. He feuded with Steinbrenner over the makeup of the roster and suffered with stress that he hadn't had to deal with as a coach. As he neared sixty, he must have wondered why he had agreed to this.

With a great second half—too little, too late—the Yankees finished third. As 1985 approached, the Yankees added the great Rickey Henderson to the roster—the man who would one day have the most stolen bases, the most runs scored, and the most leadoff home runs in history. Adding him to a team with Mattingly, Winfield, Ken Griffey Sr., Don Baylor, and Willie Randolph gave the Yankees a very strong lineup, although the season began with Mattingly, Winfield, and Henderson all recovering from injuries.

Steinbrenner backed off on criticizing Yogi and promised to trust him and not threaten to fire him. That lasted sixteen games. The Yankees won six, lost ten, and out the door Yogi went. His son Dale was crying on the team bus as they dropped his dad off at the airport following a game in Chicago, left to travel home alone.

Yogi had been given the news by general manager Clyde King. He resented the fact that Steinbrenner hadn't told him directly. For fourteen years he refused to return to Yankee Stadium, including Old-Timers' Days. He went on to coach in Houston for a few years and then retired. In his hometown in New Jersey, a Yogi Berra Museum and Learning Center was opened. Started by friends of Yogi, it helped to make people realize what a treasure he was—a man of character and integrity, someone who really lived "the Great American Dream."

A handshake at the Yogi Berra Museum and Learning Center ended a long feud between George Steinbrenner (left) and Yogi Berra over Yogi's firing in 1985. (Arthur Krasinsky / Yogi Berra Museum and Learning Center)

The love of the fans never faded—if anything, his popularity kept growing. He was quoted all the time, even by presidents, and was still one of the most recognizable people in the country. Finally, in 1999, Steinbrenner came to his museum and apologized for not firing him himself.

"I've made mistakes too," said Yogi. The feud was over.

The museum peace meeting was arranged by Suzyn Waldman, whom Steinbrenner had appointed the first female team broadcaster. By the time of the peace agreement, a new generation of Yankee announcers were in place, with Michael Kay and John Sterling as familiar to fans as Mel Allen and Red Barber had once been. After Mel and Red, Bill White (the first African-American team broadcaster), Frank Messer, and the popular Phil Rizzuto would broadcast for many years.

With Yogi's firing, guess who came back to manage? Yes, Billy Martin, for the fourth time. And this time, after he got into a public fight with pitcher Ed Whitson, he got sacked again. There was hardly anything left to say.

Rickey Henderson lived up to all expectations at first and became a crowd favorite, especially among young fans. Like Mickey Rivers (another great base runner) in the seventies, Rickey connected with younger fans, and they loved his style. When he swung and missed, he twirled his bat like a cheerleader with a baton. Rickey, whose birthday was on Christmas Day, would spend twenty-five years in the major leagues but only four and a half of them with the Yankees. He stole eighty bases in his first year with the Yankees and eighty-seven in his second. In 1988 he stole ninety-three. In 1985 he scored 146 runs in only 143 games. His 326 steals as a Yankee, even in that short time, were a club record until Derek Jeter broke it many years later.

But by 1989, Rickey seemed to lose interest in playing for the Yankees. There would be fly balls to left that he just wasn't there for. His stolen bases weren't always there when the team needed a run. Yankee fans were smart, and they saw a drop-off in effort. Some felt he needed to play for Billy Martin to be motivated, as Martin had done in both Oakland and New York. In any case, his Yankee career was all too short for the star player he was. It was unfortunate that it didn't last longer.

CHAPTER 45

Cable TV: Good for Business!

Lou Piniella came back to manage again in 1986, but the musical chairs continued a year later when he was fired and Billy Martin returned for his fifth term
as manager.

But of course, everyone knew how this would end.

The Yankees were in Texas in 1988, and Billy was in a bar. Being in Texas
brought out the worst in him, because he felt more like a cowboy looking for a
fight there than anywhere else. He said some things he shouldn't have to people
he shouldn't have, and the next thing he knew, it was the middle of the night
and he was limping into the team's hotel lobby with his ear nearly cut off and
blood all over.

This was no way for a grown man to act. It was no way for anyone to act.
Fortunately, he must have thought, it's the middle of the night and no one will
see me slither up to my room.

Bad luck. A fire alarm had rung in the hotel, and everyone had been roused
out of their rooms, in their robes or pajamas, gathering in the lobby. Just as Billy
arrived.

Somehow he survived being fired over this one, but after a second incident of throwing dirt on umpires, it was, again, time to go. Piniella finished out the season for him. One might think that the fans had had it with all of this by now, but even with seven seasons in a row out of the play-offs, the attendance that year set a team record of 2,633,701.

And this came in spite of the Mets being the hot team in town, winning the 1986 World Series and going to the play-offs three years in a row.

During the 1988 season, a big thing happened in Yankee business. They made a cable television deal so much bigger than any team had ever done—almost five hundred million dollars over the next twelve years—that suddenly, they had more money to work with than they had ever imagined.

This was the advantage of being in the biggest city in the United States. Stations could charge advertisers money based on how many people were watching, so in the biggest city, if you had a big audience, you had the highest advertising rates. The Yankees were able to make that deal, with Madison Square Garden Cable, because two other broadcast companies were trying to get the rights as well—so the bidding kept getting higher.

From that moment on, and continuing on past 2002 when the team got behind the formation of the YES Network, which they partly owned, they had more money than anyone and could spend vast amounts for free agents or to keep their own stars from leaving. People who hated the Yankees' success hated them more than ever now for assuring themselves of the most money.

But if you were a Yankee fan, all of this was great news.

Regardless of their huge new moneymaking venture, the Yankees had another disappointing finish in 1989, and the season was followed by the sad news of Billy Martin's death on Christmas Day. Martin died in an auto accident in upstate New York, and drinking was involved. Some thought he might be on the verge of returning for a sixth time as Yankee manager, but it was not to be. And so another series of managers came in and achieved little as the Yankees sank in the standings.

The Yankees couldn't seem to catch a break. Even when they had a very high draft pick, their luck turned bad. In 1990 they signed a fabulous high school pitcher named Brien Taylor. Brien's mother, Bettie, acted as his agent, and made a great deal, getting a $1,550,000 signing bonus for her son. Big things were expected, but in 1993 he got into a brawl defending his brother in a bar and dislocated his left shoulder. And yes, he threw left-handed. He was never the same, and he never got to the major leagues.

CHAPTER 46

Building from Within

The Yankees went from Piniella to Dallas Green to Bucky Dent to Stump Merrill as managers in this period, hitting last place in 1990 for only the fourth time in team history. But during the year, George Steinbrenner was suspended by the commissioner of baseball, Fay Vincent, for his actions in trying to uncover bad behavior by Dave Winfield in order to win his contract dispute against the player. He'd hired an unsavory character to "dig up dirt." It led to nothing but his suspension.

Around the same time, Gene Michael was again named the team's general manager. He had been general manager in the early eighties, but now, after years in the organization as a player, coach, manager, and scout, he was one of the most respected people in baseball, and his knowledge of the organization was extraordinary.

He proceeded to change the way the team did business—with Steinbrenner suspended, he had free rein. He had a great respect for young talent and didn't want to trade it all away to get some "quick fixes" on the team. He wanted to slow that process and develop homegrown Yankee stars when possible.

On July 7, 1991, one of those homegrown players made his major league debut. His name was Bernabe Williams, but everyone called him Bernie. Because he was soft-spoken and played classical guitar, there were some who didn't think he was "tough." He came from Puerto Rico, and not many people had paid attention to him in the minor leagues. Michael, however, saw a switch-hitter with some pop in his bat who could also cover a lot of territory in the outfield. He would become one the new building blocks toward a much improved team, and he was so impressive to Michael that the Yankees would trade their regular center fielder—Roberto Kelly—to the Cincinnati Reds, in exchange for the established Paul O'Neill.

O'Neill would quickly regain his batting form—he had slipped to .246 in 1992—and would in fact win a batting championship during his time with the

Bernie Williams's arrival in 1991 signaled the start of a new era for Yankee success.
(Charles Wenzelberg, New York Post)

Yankees. The fans took to him quickly and saw him as a warrior, which had been George Steinbrenner's word for him.

Now things were starting to fall into place. Wade Boggs, one of the great hitters in American League history, came over from Boston, also after an off year, and regained his form in New York. Jimmy Key, a free agent from Toronto, was signed by the Yankees and took his place at the top of the pitching staff. Key was a very efficient, hardworking man who had helped the Blue Jays to the world championship in 1992. As his later teammate David Wells said, "Key is one pocket protector away from full-blown nerd status, but don't let any of that fool you. He's a tough competitor."

Another acquisition was pitcher Jim Abbott, one of the great stories in baseball history. Abbott was born without a right hand, and while it made certain things difficult for him, he adjusted. He even learned to field, gracefully shifting his glove from his "bad hand" to his left hand to be in proper position if the ball was hit to him.

To Abbott, it all seemed to come easily. He was a high school star in Michigan and then a college star at the University of Michigan. He was on the United States Olympic team in the 1988 Summer Olympic Games, and then signed with the Angels. He had good seasons there before coming to the Yankees, and on September 4, 1993, he threw a no-hitter for the Yankees against the Cleveland Indians. It was one of the most inspiring moments in sports history—a player born with what many would call a severe handicap achieving a major league no-hitter.

The manager in the dugout on that September 4 afternoon, beaming with pride, was young Buck Showalter.

CHAPTER 47

Back to the Postseason

Buck was only thirty-five when he was named Yankees manager after the 1991 season. He was the youngest manager in baseball. The Yankees had gone from Bucky Dent to Stump Merrill to Buck Showalter, and since fans knew little about Buck, and he had never managed in the majors before, no one knew quite what to expect.

But he was baseball smart. He worked hard, he studied statistics, and he concentrated on his job. The game was changing; computer stats were everywhere. Buck was up for this. Players liked him. He had been a minor league teammate of Don Mattingly and would now be his manager.

He managed for five years in the Yankees' minor league system and won four titles. Gene Michael thought he had real talent as a leader.

In 1992 Buck had himself a pretty decent team. Even though Mattingly was not the player he had been, other big bats, including free agent slugger Danny Tartabull, were bringing this team back into contention. In 1993 George Steinbrenner's suspension was lifted, but by now the team was becoming more stable, more sure of itself, with a plan for winning.

The team spent some time in first place in 1993, but faded in the end as

Toronto won. Many, however, felt that the Yankees were on the verge of big things as 1994 beckoned, and a lot of sportswriters picked them to finish first. It had been thirteen years since they had done that.

Those who picked them for first knew what they were doing. The Yankees got off to a terrific start and had a 70–43 record on August 12, with a six-and-a-half game lead. These were great days to be a Yankee fan again. Fans were showing up in big numbers, wearing all sorts of Yankee clothing and caps.

And then—baseball went on strike.

It was the players' union against the owners—again—and the big issue was that the owners wanted to create a salary cap, which would keep teams from spending too much on players. Of course, the players wanted to make all they could, and they thought this was really about breaking the union, getting some players to return even without a settlement, and taking back control of the game.

The debate got so nasty that the season never resumed, and for the first time since 1904, there would be no World Series. It was just a sad end to another chapter of labor strife.

In fact, it didn't even end with the cancellation of the World Series. The strike carried into the 1995 season and caused spring training to be played by unknown substitute players, and there was a fear that the regular season might open with these no-names. But at last, in early 1995, a settlement was reached, there was no salary cap, and baseball continued.

As for 1994, the Yankees were not declared champions, but they did finish first in the season cut short to 144 games. There were no play-offs to play, no World Series to compete in, but this was very big progress.

With the strike settled in early April 1995, the Yankees gathered in Fort Lauderdale, Florida, for a shortened spring training session. It was the last gathering at Fort Lauderdale, with the team preparing to move spring training to Tampa the following year.

This spring training would be quick, getting the regular players in shape in a hurry, but four rookies managed to impress Showalter—and in doing so, wound up on the major league roster together. Would their promise show through in the season ahead?

Andy Pettitte, a rugged left-hander from Texas with piercing eyes that peered over the top of his glove as he looked in at hitters, pitched two-thirds of an inning in relief on April 29, allowing two runs and three hits.

Mariano Rivera, a starting pitcher from Panama, lost 10–0 to the Angels on May 23, giving up five runs and eight hits in three and a third innings.

Derek Jeter, the Yankees' minor league player of the year and a number one draft pick, played shortstop and batted ninth against Seattle on May 29, while going 0–5 at bat.

On September 4, Puerto Rican player Jorge Posada, whose uncle Leo had played for the Athletics, would come into the game to catch the ninth inning and make his major league debut. He did not get to bat.

The "Core Four" included (left to right) Jorge Posada, Mariano Rivera (partially hidden), Derek Jeter, and Andy Pettitte. Their "era" ran from their 1995 arrivals until Jeter's 2014 retirement. (Charles Wenzelberg, New York Post*)*

This modest start for these four players was the beginning of a remarkable run in which these same players would spend almost twenty seasons together as teammates, achieving seven pennants and five world championships and the love of a city.

And while it became the style to call them the "Core Four," which rhymed nicely, it was hard to ignore Bernie Williams, another young player from their farm system, as a fifth member of this club—he was with them for four of those championships and was just as admired.

Attendance was way down in 1995, as angry fans chose to stay home after the bitter strike. Kids even stopped buying baseball cards. Everything was suffering. A boost for baseball interest came when Lou Gehrig's amazing record of 2,130 consecutive games played fell when it was broken by Baltimore's Cal Ripken Jr. Gehrig's teammate Joe DiMaggio was at the game in Baltimore, representing the Yankees, the night the record fell. It was one highlight of a season that gave the game a lift.

But another boost for the sport was the return of the Yanks to the postseason. After fourteen years, they had made it, clinching the league's first-ever wild card slot on the final day of the season. Don Mattingly's home run against Toronto was the big hit that day. Everyone was pulling for "Donnie Baseball." He had played 1,785 games without ever getting into a postseason game. People really wanted it for him, as this felt like it would be his final season. His contract was up, and he just wasn't the player he had been. It seemed certain he wouldn't return for 1996.

To win the wild card, the Yankees won twenty-six of their last thirty-three games. David Cone, a onetime Mets star, had come through big-time, winning nine of eleven down the stretch.

The wild card play-off series would be against the Seattle Mariners, led by their very gifted outfield star Ken Griffey Jr. Griffey Sr. had played for the Yankees in the 1980s and had finished his career as a teammate of Junior's. That had never before happened in baseball. (One day they hit back-to-back home runs.)

Junior did not like the Yankees, because Billy Martin had yelled at him when he was a kid visiting the clubhouse with his dad.

The Yankees were wearing a number 7 on their sleeves in honor of the great Mickey Mantle, who had died in August following treatment for cancer.

They won the first two play-off games at Yankee Stadium, taking the second one when Jim Leyritz hit a home run in the fifteenth inning. It was 1:22 in the morning when he smacked it. What a big hit for Leyritz, who seemed to specialize in big hits.

Then it was on to Seattle, where the Mariners won two in a row to tie the series and set up a final game. It was win or go home. And what a game it was!

In the last of the eighth, Griffey hit his fifth home run of the series to cut the Yankees' lead to 4–3. The Mariners tied it, and into extra innings they went. The two relief pitchers now were Randy Johnson, the great ace of the Mariners staff, and Jack McDowell, a newcomer to the Yankees but a longtime star in the American League.

In the top of the eleventh inning, Randy Velarde, a utility infielder for New York, singled home a run to give the Yanks a 5–4 lead. But in the last of the eleventh, the great DH Edgar Martinez doubled home two runs, the winning run being a sliding Griffey, and the Mariners were moving on. In fact, the excitement in Seattle helped the voters pass a bill that approved construction of Safeco Field and would keep the Mariners from moving. If Yankee Stadium was the House that Ruth Built, Safeco was the House that Griffey Built!

The Yankees, though, were going home.

It didn't take George Steinbrenner long to take action over this disappointment. He fired Buck Showalter a few days later. "He knows the bottom line," said Steinbrenner. And the bottom line on the Yankees was to win it all.

Mattingly hit .417 in the series, including his last home run—a very emotional moment for Yankee fans. But his career was over. He had a .307 lifetime average, would have his number 23 retired and a plaque in Monument Park, but the Yankees would be turning to a new first baseman for 1996.

And of course, they would also need a new manager.

His name was Joe Torre.

CHAPTER 48

Joe Torre

No one knew at the time, but the hiring of Joe Torre would lead to a new era of Yankee greatness and would send Torre to the Baseball Hall of Fame.

Not only did no one know it, but the *New York Daily News* headline after he was hired said, CLUELESS JOE.

It was intended to mean that Joe had no idea what he was getting into. But it was read by many as saying, "Here is nice guy Joe Torre, born in Brooklyn, a very good player in his time, but a manager who had failed to produce a championship with the Mets, with the Braves, or with the Cardinals." Everyone liked Joe, he was a "regular guy," but he simply hadn't done very well as a manager.

Until now.

A lot of things changed for the Yankees when Joe Torre arrived. The team moved its spring training base to Tampa, Florida. The ground crew learned to smooth out the infield in the sixth inning to the rhythm of the recorded *YMCA* song by the Village People, which the fans in Yankee Stadium came to love. Torre hired the roly-poly Don "the Gerbil" Zimmer as his bench coach. Zimmer was

Brooklyn-born Joe Torre led the Yankees to four world championships between 1996 and 2000.
(Charles Wenzelberg, New York Post)

a great choice—he had a knack for spotting things on the field that could make the difference in a game.

Tino Martinez came from Seattle to take over first base from Mattingly. It was not going to be easy for anyone to replace Mattingly in the hearts of Yankee fans, but Tino proved he was up to it. He had a great Yankee Stadium swing, hit a lot of home runs, drove in a lot of runs—and, well, fans had to admit that they were unlikely to get that kind of production from Mattingly with his bad back. His time had passed, but at least he had gone out with a big play-off series in fans' memories.

One problem for the Yankees was at shortstop. Who was going to play there? Tony Fernandez broke his elbow, and it wasn't going to be him. The Yankees thought Derek Jeter was going to be their shortstop of the future—but was 1996 his year? Was he ready?

A lot of people in the Yankee front office thought they needed to go out and get a veteran shortstop as protection, in case Jeter needed another year in the minor leagues. He was only twenty-one years old. Did he have what it took to perform at such an important position at Yankee Stadium?

For a time, a trade was considered. There was a shortstop on Seattle who might be available. His name was Felix Fermin, and he was a thirty-one-year-old veteran. What would it take to get him in a Yankee uniform?

A deal could be made. All the Yankees had to do was give Seattle a pitcher in return. Maybe a starter named Bob Wickman.

Or maybe a reliever named Mariano Rivera.

That is how easily baseball history could change. The Yankees could have traded Rivera to get a fill-in shortstop for protection. Fermin could have had a good year, and maybe the Yankees could have traded Jeter, knowing they were in good hands.

Fortunately for the Yankees, Gene Michael and others decided to go with Jeter and turn down the Fermin trade. Rivera would stay with the Yankees and would become an important setup man for closer John Wetteland in 1996. Some people even thought he was the team's most valuable player in that role, pretty much shutting down the opponent's chances by the seventh or eighth innings.

Jeter was a well-mannered young man who'd been born in New Jersey but raised in Kalamazoo, Michigan. He was a Yankees fan, largely because he spent summers visiting his grandmother in New Jersey and watching the Yankees on TV. As he learned to play ball, he imagined himself one day playing for the Yankees. It was his dream.

His mother was white, and his father was black. He did not seem to suffer from any bullying that might have gone on because of his mixed heritage, and if anyone felt that way, he could answer on the baseball fields, where he was clearly destined for greatness.

Jeter took over as shortstop and never looked back. It soon became apparent that his strong arm and great range would make him one of the best in baseball.

In fact, after only a few seasons, it was clear that he was going to be the best shortstop in Yankees history.

Yankees captain Derek Jeter gave the Yankees twenty seasons as the greatest shortstop in team history.
(Charles Wenzelberg, New York Post)

He could run back on balls and throw like a quarterback to first base even from the grass in short left field. These became regular Jeter plays as the fans watched in amazement. His smile was always there in the dugout, sometimes when he would rub Zimmer's bald head for good luck. He never said anything he wished he could take back. He would play ball in New York for two decades and managed to maintain a high standard of conduct even with the tough New York press looking after his every move.

Derek had it all. By 2003 he would be named team captain, and for his entire time with the Yankees, he was the Man. He played hard every game and led by example. If there was a TV commercial featuring a baseball player, he was likely to be that player. He was, in a way, the face of major league baseball—a very positive role model. And he was a great clutch hitter—the player opponents did not want to see at bat with the game on the line.

He was the guy who parents wanted their kids to grow up to be, much like Lou Gehrig many years before.

In 1996 he was on his way to a Rookie of the Year season and the Yankees were on their way to the Eastern Division title. This would be Joe Torre's first shot at a World Series in his long career, which he'd started as a minor league player in 1960 and as a manager in 1977. Joe was an emotional guy too—people rooted hard for him. His sister was a nun who attended most Yankee home games. His brother Frank, a former major leaguer, received a heart transplant during the Yankees' postseason, and everyone rooted for the Torre brothers.

Suddenly this team was hard to hate. A lot of people who rooted for other clubs seemed to always hate the Yankees, but with Torre, Jeter, Bernie Williams, Tino Martinez, Rivera—it was hard to root against these guys. They honored both their team and the game of baseball with the way they played, showing not only great talent but humility and dignity. And of course, the Yankees had been down for a long time. Baseball always seemed to have its biggest years—attendance, television ratings, etc.—when the Yankees were hot.

The Yankees beat Texas in the division series and then took on Baltimore. In the first game, Jeter hit one that seemed headed for the first row in right field. The Orioles' right fielder, Tony Tarasco, felt he could catch it, perhaps by leaping high to the top of the wall.

But wait. Standing at the front row was twelve-year-old Jeffrey Maier, a Yankee fan from New Jersey, there with his family to take in the game. And young Jeffrey, wearing a glove, reached out and pulled the ball into the stands. He didn't catch it—he deflected it to another fan—but umpire Rich Garcia ruled it a home run. It tied the game, and a Bernie home run in the eleventh inning won it for New York.

Tarasco—and his Orioles teammates—went crazy over the call. Interference! Interference! But Garcia stuck to his call. (He later admitted he had blown it, and a replay rule, which took effect in 2008, would have changed the call.)

As for young Jeffrey Maier, his name became part of Yankees history.

The Yankees went on to win the series against Baltimore, and then came the Atlanta Braves. The World Series.

The Yanks were down two games to one and losing the fourth game 6–3 going to the eighth inning. They were close to being down three games to one. But then Jim Leyritz, acting again as Mr. Clutch, powered one over the left-field wall to tie the score. They won in the tenth, and behind rookie Andy Pettitte, they won game five 1–0. In game six, their catcher, Joe Girardi, hustled out a big triple to spark the team to their twenty-third world championship—and its first in eighteen years.

What a postseason! The Jeffrey Maier play, the Leyritz homer, the Pettitte shutout, the Girardi triple! It was an amazing finish. Third baseman Wade Boggs jumped onto a police horse after the game as the Yankees celebrated on the field. Torre, a winner at last, had tears in his eyes as he waved to his family in the stands.

Bob Watson became the first African-American general manager to win a World Series. He would stay with the team for one more season, before turning the job over to thirty-year-old Brian Cashman in 1998. Cashman would be the youngest general manager in Yankee history and would go on to a very long run in the job, learning as he went along and becoming one of the most respected executives in the game.

The Yanks turned over the job of closer from John Wetteland to Mariano Rivera in 1997. From what people could tell, Rivera had what it took for the job, which was both mentally and physically challenging. But he also had an amazing "cutter," a pitch that seemed to break up, not down, the way gravity

Mariano Rivera's brilliance as a closer led to 652 saves plus 42 more in postseason play.
(*Charles Wenzelberg,* New York Post)

intended baseballs to travel. With that pitch, Rivera would go on to a Hall of Fame career with the most saves in baseball history.

But since he was usually out on the mound with the game on the line, sometimes things didn't work out. And one of those times was in the division series of 1997, when Cleveland's Sandy Alomar Jr. hit a game-tying home run off Rivera when the Yankees were just four outs away from moving on to the next round. The Yankees lost the game, and their season ended right there. But Rivera, who believed deeply in the Bible and that things good and bad happen for a reason, overcame the setback and prepared himself to come back in 1998 and do his best. One of his great strengths was his ability to accept the occasional failure and be ready the next time he was called upon.

When baseball fans talk about the "greatest team ever," there are four Yankee teams that come up for consideration. The 1927 Yankees usually are the first one mentioned, but they are joined by the 1939 team, the 1961 team—and now, the 1998 team.

What a year that was. Trades brought Scott Brosius to play third and Chuck Knoblauch to play second, and on a pitching staff loaded with top players like Pettitte and David Cone, three others gained a lot of attention.

First there was Orlando Hernandez, nicknamed "El Duque," a Cuban pitcher who escaped that country on a small boat and quickly wound up in the Yankees rotation, wowing fans and even opponents with tremendous stuff.

A lot of terrific players came from Latin America—meaning Puerto Rico, Dominican Republic, Venezuela, Panama, and Mexico. Players there could play year-round and really develop their skills. The Cuban people loved baseball, but Cuba and the United States had not maintained diplomatic relations for almost forty years, so players could not move easily from that island nation near Florida to the United States, where big money might await them. El Duque, a star player on their national team, had to sneak out under cover of darkness to make it to America. And El Duque became almost a magical figure with his brilliance on the mound.

Then there was the Yankees' first Japanese player, a half-American pitcher named Hideki Irabu. Although he had a decent record of 13–9, Irabu was not a good signing by the Yankees in coming years, and fans began to joke that his name was pronounced "I-rob-you."

And then there was oversize David Wells, who had great control over his pitches but not his waistline. He weighed over three hundred pounds at some portions of his career. He was a colorful character whose mother was in a motorcycle gang. Wells was also a memorabilia collector, and he once purchased—and wore in a game—a Yankees cap worn by Babe Ruth. (Since it was flat as a pancake and looked different from his teammates' caps, the umpires made him remove it.)

On May 17, Wells put his name into baseball history books by pitching the first perfect game by a Yankee since Don Larsen had done it in the 1956 World Series. What was amazing was that Larsen and Wells had attended the same high school in San Diego, California.

The story became even more remarkable a year later, when, also on a Sunday afternoon, David Cone pitched another Yankee perfect game. Here were two guys named David pitching perfect games a year apart, both in Yankee Stadium and both on Sunday afternoons. To further make the Cone perfect game magical, Larsen happened to throw out the ceremonial first pitch that afternoon, which was Yogi Berra Day. Yogi, borrowing Joe Girardi's glove, caught the pitch. So there was Girardi, catching the Cone perfect game, using a glove worn by Berra for the first pitch. Yogi, of course, had caught Larsen's gem in 1956.

Crazy things could certainly happen at Yankee Stadium—and did!

But 1998 was really something special. Including the postseason, which led to a World Championship, the Yankees won 125 games and lost only fifty. It seemed

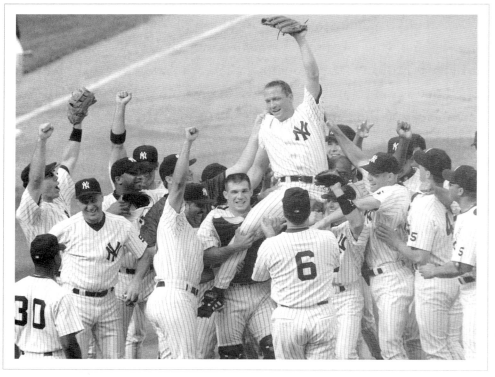

David Cone is hoisted after his 1999 perfect game. His catcher, Joe Girardi (center), went on to manage the team. Number 30 is coach Willie Randolph, a Yankee great as a player, and he is facing coach Mel Stottlemyre, who threw forty shutouts for the team. Over Stottlemyre's left shoulder is Cuban import Orlando "El Duque" Hernandez. Joe Torre is number 6. (Bob Olen, New York Post)

like everything they did worked out. They brought up a rookie named Shane Spencer late in the season, one of the spring training replacement players from the 1994–95 strike. He had sixty-seven at bats, but he hit ten home runs, three of them grand slams.

In 1998, Roger Maris's record of sixty-one home runs fell to Mark McGwire and Sammy Sosa, both of whom, it came to be believed, had used steroids (performance-enhancing drugs). But it didn't matter about individual records to the '98 Yanks. No one on the team hit more than twenty-eight home runs, but they had 207 as a team, and it seemed like each day, they could be losing 5–3 or 4–0, and fans would know they would win. The bull pen would stop the opponents cold in the later innings, while the bats kept pounding out hits.

When the season was over, free agent Bernie Williams had an offer to go to the Red Sox. But his heart wasn't in it. He felt like he was a Yankee for life, and even though the Yankees didn't want to give him a seven-year contract, they didn't want to lose him to their biggest rival. And so they signed Bernie and he would be a Yankee for life, just like Gehrig, Dickey, DiMaggio, Ford, and Mantle, and just like Jeter, Posada, and Rivera would be. It was a very exclusive club, and Yogi Berra always kicked himself for playing four games for the Mets in 1965 and removing himself from that list. (There were others, like Combs, Crosetti, Rolfe, Rizzuto, Henrich, McDougald, Richardson, Kubek, Stottlemyre, Guidry, and Mattingly, but it was still a small list.)

Also at the end of the '98 season, the Yankees made an enormous trade with Toronto, dealing their star pitcher David Wells to the Blue Jays for the great Roger Clemens.

Clemens had long been an archrival with Boston, but he had moved on to the Blue Jays as a free agent and won the Cy Young Award there. Now he would be a Yankee. For some Yankee fans, who had long rooted against him, it was a little hard to accept the Rocket in pinstripes. But he turned out to be a great teammate, well liked in the clubhouse, and still a terrific pitcher—even if, some years later, his name was also linked to steroid use.

CHAPTER 49

Team of the Century

Joe DiMaggio died on March 8, 1999. He had been honored by a special day devoted to him at the end of the '98 season, but he was already ill with cancer by then and suffering from pneumonia as well. (He also had pneumonia when they had a Joe DiMaggio Day in 1949.)

This was forty-eight years after he played his last game, and his fans—the ones who grew up idolizing him—were growing fewer in number. He was better known to younger fans through his television commercials. He always represented class and style. He was awarded the Presidential Medal of Freedom, would have his own US postage stamp, and was always the main attraction wherever he appeared. In his honor, the 1999 Yankees would wear a number 5 on their sleeves and would have a memorial where Paul Simon sang his famous line, "Where have you gone, Joe DiMaggio" from Simon & Garfunkel's "Mrs. Robinson."

Cancer seemed to haunt the team in 1999. Joe Torre had prostate cancer and missed the first thirty-six games of the season recovering from successful surgery, while Zimmer filled in. Darryl Strawberry, a slugging outfielder, was diagnosed with colon cancer, and on top of that was suspended by major league baseball for illegal narcotics use.

Darryl, along with his old New York Mets teammate Doc Gooden, were both in and out of trouble during their careers, but George Steinbrenner signed them both and got productive performances from them, including a no-hitter by Gooden. So long as a player could help the Yankees—and showed a willingness to deal with the issues that surrounded them—George Steinbrenner was prepared to offer a helping hand. In the end, Straw and Doc were positive forces on the Yankees, even as their addictions ultimately brought them down.

The fans loved the way the Yankees played in this period, and in 1999 more than three million turned out—the first time that had happened in Yankee history. They again won the division and the division series but had to go against a tough Red Sox team in the League Championship Series.

Yogi Berra, just a visitor now, walked into the Yankees clubhouse before that series began. He saw some worried looks.

"What's wrong?" he asked Bernie Williams.

"Oh, it's a tough week we're facing," said Bernie. "Those guys are good."

Yogi looked at him and said, "Don't worry . . . these guys have been trying to beat us for eighty years."

Bernie laughed. Yogi was right. He always was. Williams relaxed, and went out and helped his team knock off the Red Sox—and then swept the Braves in four straight, to win the World Series for the twenty-fifth time. It was the last year of the twentieth century. In the last seventy-nine years, the Yankees had won thirty-six pennants. No one else came close. They were, no doubt, the "Team of the Century."

Jorge Posada took over as the Yankees' regular catcher in 2000. He was "old school" in the dedication he brought to each game, and in his habit of never wearing batting gloves. Yankee fans took to shouting "Hip hip Jorge!" when he came to bat. Posada could often be seen walking to the mound to "talk some serious sense" into his pitchers. He really was an on-field manager, and was well schooled by his mentor, Joe Girardi, for whom he had been a backup catcher.

The 2000 Yankees won again—a third straight pennant, and then they followed it with a third straight World Series win. In the Series, against the Mets, they ran their winning streak in World Series games to fourteen.

This was a "subway series," Yankees versus Mets, the first subway series since the Yankees played the Brooklyn Dodgers in 1956. It was called a subway series because fans could get to both stadiums by subway. It was an exciting time to be a baseball fan in New York. Everyone wore their shirts and caps to show their loyalties. People matched up the two teams, position by position. The managers, Bobby Valentine of the Mets and Torre, were both local residents with tons of friends in town. Maybe the rest of the country didn't care—the series had very low TV ratings—but New York was going crazy with Yankees against the Mets!

This was a World Series that saw Mariano Rivera break Whitey Ford's record for consecutive shutout innings in World Series play (he would run his streak up to thirty-four and one-third), but more strangely, a play by Roger Clemens that left even Yankee fans baffled.

Roger "the Rocket" Clemens was 20–3 for the 2001 Yankees. (Charles Wenzelberg, New York Post)

Clemens seemed to have a personal feud with the Mets' slugger Mike Piazza. Once during an interleague game (interleague play had begin in 1997), Clemens had beaned Piazza with a hard fastball to the helmet. This followed a grand slam home run by Piazza off Clemens.

Now, in this World Series game, Piazza shattered his bat in the first inning of game two. The ball went foul, but Piazza ran it out just the same. On his way to first, Clemens picked up a piece of the broken bat and threw it at him.

Piazza, and the fans, wondered what in the world had just taken place. Clemens's explanation was that he was so focused on the play, he mistook the piece of bat for the ball. Few people could buy that.

With that odd explanation, people were still wondering what he could have been thinking.

Regardless of that bizarre incident, the Yankees won the World Series in five games. Bragging rights in New York were theirs!

CHAPTER 50

A World Series After 9/11

If the Yankees could win the World Series in 2001, they would have four in a row, and they'd be in position to go after their own record of five straight the following year.

Roger Clemens went 20–3 at the age of thirty-eight to lead a pitching staff that now included Mike Mussina, obtained from Baltimore via free agency. They also had a new second baseman, Alfonso Soriano, who stole forty-three bases and hit eighteen home runs. Soriano came from the small village of San Pedro de Macoris in the Dominican Republic, which had come to be considered as a hotbed for talented infielders. Soriano would be one of the better ones.

Soriano had also played in Japan, so he was a rare ballplayer who could speak Spanish, English, and Japanese.

The Yankees got him mostly because their second baseman Chuck Knoblauch, had developed a case of the "yips." For reasons impossible to understand, poor Chuck had lost his ability to throw straight to first base. He must have psyched himself out; it was probably mental, of course. The Yankees moved him to left field and put Soriano at second.

The Yankees were in their usual position of first place on September 11 when the city of New York suffered the worst day in its history. On that sunny summer morning, as people began arriving at work, two hijacked jets hit the World Trade Center towers in lower Manhattan. Both buildings burst into flames and ultimately collapsed to the ground, killing almost three thousand people, including many police officers and firefighters who were there as first responders.

Baseball came to a halt. America was under attack, and baseball would have to wait.

Yankee players visited injured rescue workers at the hospital, visited families at an armory who were identifying loved ones, and visited rescue workers at the Javits Convention Center. They did what they could while baseball took a backseat to the tragedy.

Bernie Williams came up to one woman who was desperately looking for the remains of her husband.

"I don't know what to say," he told her. "All I know is, I think you need a hug."

That small gesture was part of the healing process in New York that was about to begin. Baseball would play a role in it. Yankee Stadium would serve as the site of a huge memorial service, and when the Yankees resumed play in Chicago a week later, Chicago fans wore New York caps and cheered for the Yankees, just to show support for the city. "God Bless America," a World War I–era song that captured the rising patriotism in a city so shattered, would be played in the seventh inning at Yankee Stadium.

When the Yankees won the Eastern Division, there was no champagne sprayed on teammates. It was still a sad time in New York, and the Yankees players lifted their glasses in a toast and avoided a big celebration.

In the division series against Oakland, Derek Jeter made a play for the ages when he left his position and dashed to the right of home plate in case a throw from left field was wild. It was, and Jeter was right there. In one motion, he flipped it to Posada, who tagged out the Oakland runner to preserve a Yankee lead. "The Flip" became one of the famous plays of baseball history. No one could remember ever seeing an infielder making such a smart play.

The Yankees beat Oakland and played Seattle in the League Championship Series. Seattle had won 116 games in the regular season—a record—but the Yankees took this series too, aided by a dramatic walk-off home run in the fourth game by Soriano.

Now came the World Series, and it seemed like the whole country was rooting for New York, just because of the grief the country still felt over the 9/11 attack.

The Yankees' opponent was the Arizona Diamondbacks, an expansion team in only its fourth season of play.

The D-backs lost the first two games in Arizona, and the Yankees came home to find President George W. Bush on hand to throw out the ceremonial first pitch. He warmed up under the stands before the game. When Jeter saw him, he said, "Hey, Mr. President, are you going to throw from the mound or from in front of it?"

The president asked Jeter what he thought. "Throw from the mound," he said, "or else they'll boo you. But don't bounce it. They'll boo you."

Despite wearing a bulletproof vest under his suit, and with the warnings of Jeter in his mind, the president threw a strike. Somehow, it lifted a nation's spirits. Baseball can do that. It was a great moment for the sport and for the recovering city.

There were some "miracle moments" in the Series. In game four, with the Yankees trailing 3–1 in the bottom of the ninth, Tino Martinez belted a two-out, two-run homer to tie the score. What a moment for Tino!

Then, in the last of the tenth, as the clock struck midnight on November 1, Derek Jeter homered down the right-field line to win the game.

A fan held up a sign that said, MR. NOVEMBER. How did that fan know to bring that sign?

The next night, game five, was just as dramatic, if that was possible. It began with Paul O'Neill in right field hearing the fans chanting his name as tears formed in his eyes. Everyone seemed to know that he would be retiring after the Series and that this would be his last game in Yankee Stadium.

"Paul O-Neill . . . Paul O-Neill . . . Paul O-Neill," yelled the fans. Paul couldn't believe it. What a player he had been for this team.

With the Series now tied at 2–2, the game was tied 2–2 after third baseman Scott Brosius hit a two-run homer in the bottom of the ninth. It was off the same pitcher who had given up the Jeter homer the night before, Byung-Hyun Kim.

In the twelfth inning, Soriano got a game-winning single, and the Series returned to Arizona with the Yanks up 3–2 after two miracle victories. And the nation was pulling for the Yankees!

But it didn't work out the way a Hollywood scriptwriter would want it. Arizona won twice at home, with the final game decided on a bloop single by Arizona's Luis Gonzalez with the infield drawn in. Mariano Rivera gave up the hit, and the Yankees lost. The streak of three straight world championships was over. But what a run they had given it in this thrilling World Series.

And after it was over, O'Neill and Brosius retired, and Tino Martinez went to the Cardinals as a free agent. It was the end of the run that brought five pennants and four world championships in Joe Torre's first six years as manager.

CHAPTER 51

A Difficult Time for Baseball

By 2002, baseball had to face up to its whispered problem of steroid use by some of its players.

The use of these performance-enhancing drugs had been quietly discussed for about ten years. Barry Bonds's seventy-three home runs in 2001—along with his enlarged head and pro wrestler build—was making this a subject that could not be overlooked.

Ken Caminiti, a former Most Valuable Player, talked about his steroid use in *Sports Illustrated*—and died not long afterward. Jose Canseco was quite open about his usage as well and wrote a book naming suspected users.

The drugs may have given some players extra performance, but they were not legal, and there were serious health hazards connected with them. But the users were getting big contracts, and the players who were clean were losing their jobs to the "juicers." It was a very bad time for the game, and everyone seemed to carry some blame—the players who used them, the players who kept quiet about it, the Players Association (the union for baseball players) for refusing to enter into a testing agreement, Major League Baseball for seemingly not taking the issue seriously, and the media, who knew what was going on but did not report on it very much.

And yet, it was defining an era—the Steroid Era—in which the record book was being rewritten by hitters and pitchers—mostly hitters—who were piling up big numbers while using illegal performance enhancers.

The Yankees were no better than any other team when it came to performance-enhancing drug usage. Their big first baseman, Jason Giambi, who signed a seven-year contract in 2002 to replace Tino Martinez, had times of great success and great failure, all of which seemed linked to steroids, which he finally admitted to. The great Roger Clemens wound up being charged with steroid use. Andy Pettitte, Clemens's close friend, admitted to using the drugs to try to recover from an injury.

In 2006 an agreement was reached between MLB and the Players Association that permitted testing, although the results would at first be secret. At the end of 2007, the Mitchell Report was issued by the baseball commissioner's office, and it named names. Eventually, those failing the tests would be revealed and not kept secret. They would be suspended for a minimum of fifty games for a first offense. The game was going to be cleaner, but there were still players who were finding ways to beat the testing. Baseball would always have to find ways to keep up with them.

With each new season, suspicions rose and records continued to fall. The Yankees had their share of players in the Mitchell Report, but the whole game was affected, no single team.

In 2002 the Yankees brought back David Wells and added Giambi, but the team got knocked out in the first round of the play-offs.

The year 2003 was the team's hundredth anniversary season, and they added one of the great players in Japanese history, Hideki Matsui. Matsui would be the first Japanese everyday player signed by the Yankees, and what a great signing he would be. Although he did not speak English, the fans saw him as a man who

Hideki Matsui was a fan favorite despite never mastering English. He was the MVP of the 2009 World Series. (Charles Wenzelberg, New York Post)

played the game hard, with modesty, honor, and dignity. He gave his all every day. He played 518 consecutive games for the Yankees from the day he arrived, the team's longest streak since Lou Gehrig, and the longest streak to start a professional baseball career in US history. He would have some very big seasons for the Yankees and would become one of their most popular players.

His nickname in Japan was "Godzilla," after a Japanese science fiction movie series, but the nickname never became that popular in the United States, because somehow it seemed a little insulting to such a fine person. And so New York fans learned to say Hideki Matsui, bought his number 55 T-shirts, and gave him tremendous respect.

Without ever doing an English language interview, he became an all-time Yankee.

CHAPTER 52

Aaron Boone Connects

On July 31, 2003, the Yankees made a trade with Cincinnati to get third base-man Aaron Boone. Boone was one of just three players in baseball history whose father *and* grandfather had played in the majors. Boone was not a big star, but a big day was coming for him.

The Yankees faced the Red Sox in the American League Championship Series after putting away the Twins in the first round. This was, as usual, a highly competitive matchup between these two big rivals, and the rivalry got even bigger when a fight broke out in the third game in which Pedro Martinez, the Red Sox star pitcher, shoved Yankee bench coach Don Zimmer to the ground after Zim charged onto the field angrily, looking for Martinez. The sight of the seventy-two-year-old overweight Zim crashing to the ground was scary. Martinez later apologized, but Zim said, "What does he have to apologize for? I was the guy who charged him and threw the punch!"

The series went down to a game seven in Yankee Stadium. Mariano Rivera pitched three shutout innings—a very rare outing for him—as the game went into extra innings. The winner would go to the World Series; everything was on the line.

In the eighth inning, Boone went in as a pinch runner, and he stayed in the game to play third. He came to bat in the last of the eleventh inning to hit against the tough knuckleballer pitcher Tim Wakefield. His brother Bret Boone, also a player, was one of the announcers in the broadcast booth.

Taking his first at bat of the long night, at 12:16 in the morning, Boone blasted one to deep left, and into the seats it went for a pennant-winning home run! It was right there with Bucky Dent and Chris Chambliss in historic Yankee home runs. The Yankees were going to the World Series; the Red Sox were going home.

The Yankees lost the World Series to the upstart Florida Marlins, but the Boone moment was the postseason moment to remember.

But now events started to turn.

First Boone tore a ligament in his knee playing pickup basketball in February 2004. He would be lost for the season.

Desperate to find a replacement, the Yankees swung a huge deal, sending Soriano, their fine second baseman, to the Texas Rangers for Alex Rodriguez. "A-Rod" was a shortstop, but the Yankees had Jeter at shortstop, so he agreed to move to third base to replace Boone.

CHAPTER 53

A-Rod and Cano

With A-Rod the Yankees got perhaps the best player in the game, a man who had led the league in home runs all three years he was in Texas, after spending his first seven seasons with Seattle. In 2001, Texas signed him to a remarkable $252 million, ten-year contract, and now they were happy to find another team—the Yankees—to relieve them of that.

Rodriguez was born just a few miles from Yankee Stadium in the Washington Heights section of Manhattan, a largely Dominican community. It was the neighborhood where the Yankees were born, playing in old Hilltop Park.

He was raised in Miami and played his first major league game at age eighteen. He had enormous gifts, but it turned out that he was using steroids during his time in Texas. At the Yankees' spring training camp in 2009, he confessed that he'd turned to them "because of all the pressure on me after that big contract." He swore that since playing in Texas, he had been clean.

Major league baseball loved the handsome A-Rod because he seemed on the path to breaking Barry Bonds's career home run record (not so clean), and the news that he too had used steroids was very disappointing. He was so talented without them! He had it all!

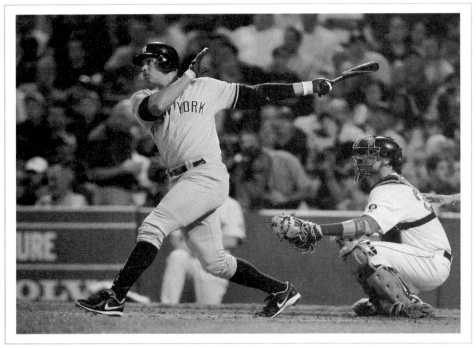

Alex Rodriguez won two MVP awards while playing for the Yankees but often found himself surrounded by controversy, including some for his use of performance-enhancing drugs. (Charles Wenzelberg, New York Post)

A-Rod dated stars like Cameron Diaz, Kate Hudson, and Madonna, and he enjoyed the glamour of being a Yankee. His friendship with Jeter, once considered very solid, was not so strong now that they were teammates. They were once bonded by being two of the best young players in the game, and they enjoyed getting together. Now, perhaps Jeter suspected that A-Rod was continuing to use steroids, or perhaps their different personalities couldn't hold up to friendship once they were together every day.

But make no mistake about it, A-Rod was still a really great player. He won two MVP awards while with the Yankees. In 2007 he hit fifty-four home runs and drove in 156 runs in 158 games. Who does things like that? Only a player on a very, very elite level. And this was a player who drove in more than a hundred runs fourteen times in his first fifteen full seasons, including eleven in a row. Did fans suspect his performance was related to steroid use? Some did, but most preferred to think it was natural talent, since he had been a spectacular player long before steroids had crept into the game. He was hardly a sudden sensation once they began to appear.

In his first Yankee season, 2004, the team fell short in a bad way. Oh, it had been a good regular season, which included an all-out play by Jeter in a big game against Boston in which he dove into the stands and came out with a bloodied face and bruises—but caught the ball.

But after winning the first three games of the American League Championship Series against the Red Sox, and seemingly on their way to the World Series again, the unthinkable happened. The team shut down. Boston won one, two, three, four in a row—the first time that had ever happened in postseason baseball history. The Yanks were knocked out, and four World Series games later, the Red Sox stood on top of the world, breaking the "Curse of the Bambino" and winning their first world championship since 1918.

It was a tough time to be a Yankee fan. The Red Sox finally had bragging rights and had finally shut down the curse that went back to their sale of Babe Ruth to New York. And they did it by knocking off the Yankees head-to-head.

Still, adding Alex Rodriguez was for many years a good deal for the Yankees (they did not have to pay his full salary; Texas contributed to it), but it did leave second base worse off with Soriano gone.

In May 2005, Joe Torre turned over second base to a Dominican rookie named Robinson Cano. He came from the same town as Soriano.

Cano wore number 24, the reverse of his namesake Jackie Robinson's 42. Cano's father had briefly pitched for Houston in 1989 (the team where Clemens and Pettitte had now relocated to as free agents). Cano's performance in the major leagues was nothing like his minor league record—it was a lot better. Not too many players can ever say such a thing.

At first Cano was tucked into the lineup just as a way of showing some

Robinson Cano was named after Jackie Robinson and gave the Yankees nine great seasons at second base. He then became one of the few homegrown Yankees to leave via free agency. (Charles Wenzelberg, New York Post*)*

improvement at second. But as the years passed, it was hard to deny that he might have been the best second baseman in the Yankees history. He hit for power, he hit for average, and in the field, he made it look so easy, especially when he would whip the ball to first without appearing to be exerting any effort.

He was durable—he almost never missed a game—and he was dependable. And for a few years, with A-Rod, Jeter, and Cano playing, the Yankees appeared to have their best third baseman, shortstop, and second baseman out there at the same time. After more than a hundred years and all those great players, that was amazing. (Of course, Lou Gehrig was their greatest first baseman.)

Despite their all-star lineup, the Yankees got knocked out of the play-offs by the Angels again in 2005—and by the Tigers in 2006 and the Indians in 2007. They drew more than four million fans in each of those seasons but fell short of the World Series each time. This was not the way George Steinbrenner wanted things.

Steinbrenner, growing older, was letting his sons get more involved in running the team. He used to call it "letting the young elephants into the tent." He wasn't the only one growing older—many of the players were, and the ballpark was. There was more and more talk about building a new Yankee Stadium, and finally it was going to happen. The year 2008 would be the last year of the "old Yankee Stadium," and 2009 would see the opening of a new one right across the street in the Bronx.

The new Yankee Stadium (far left) is shown under construction next to the original stadium (remodeled in 1976) not far from the Harlem River. (Wilson F. Turner)

CHAPTER 54

Attack of the Midges!

For years there had been talk of the Yankees moving. Maybe to New Jersey, or maybe to the west side of Manhattan. But the financing wasn't there, and the public did not want to pay for a new stadium. At last, by 2006, the team had figured out a way to finance it themselves, and that would be the plan.

Meanwhile, on they played, looking for that magic formula, that winning combination to put them back in the Series. Big stars like Gary Sheffield, Kevin Brown, and Randy Johnson came and went, some producing, some failing. Roger Clemens surprised everyone by un-retiring, but not adding much. His buddy Andy Pettitte returned too and pitched until 2010, retired, and then returned to finish in 2013. Had he not pitched those three years in Houston, he would likely have passed Whitey Ford as the winningest pitcher in Yankee history.

A Japanese pitcher named Kei Igawa was an awful failure. A pitcher named Cory Lidle was killed after the 2006 season when his small plane crashed into a Manhattan apartment building, bringing back sad memories of Thurman Munson's death.

A star pitcher from Taiwan, Chien-Ming Wang, won nineteen games two years in a row before hurting himself as a base runner and never rediscovering his form. His name was pronounced "Wong," but Jeter would always see him in the clubhouse and say, "Wassup, Wanger?" Jeter made everyone feel welcome.

Joba Chamberlain burst on the scene in 2007. A beefy Native American, he was raised by a single father who also happened to be handicapped and would play catch with him from his wheelchair. Joba made nineteen appearances after getting called up from the minors, and he allowed only one run in all those games. He looked a little like Babe Ruth on the mound and just blew the competition away. His career never quite reached that level again, but in that rookie season, he was remembered for being on the mound in a play-off game at Cleveland, when flying insects attacked the players on the field.

The insects were called midges, and the sight of them swarming onto the Yankee players, hanging on to their bodies, and making the play miserable, haunted the team. Torre called it his biggest mistake ever—not removing his team from the field. No matter what was sprayed on the players, the midges stayed. And the Yankees lost the game, and the series.

A-Rod had become a distraction. Even though he was making so much money, he was entitled to "opt out" of his contract and get a new one starting in 2008. A lot of fans were turned off by his poor postseason performances and were ready to say good-bye. But the Yankees wanted him back, wanted his special talents wearing the Yankee uniform, especially since it still looked like he would one day become the all-time home run king.

So the Yanks gave him a new ten-year contract for $275 million that would keep him a Yankee through the 2017 season. And he would get bonus payments each time he passed someone on the all-time home run list.

Joe Torre was still enormously popular with the fans—and maybe the greatest manager in Yankee history—but when he got knocked out of the 2007 play-offs, it marked four years in a row without a World Series appearance. The Yankees counted on getting to the Series to make the additional money that the Series provided, and to help pay the big contracts of their big stars.

Some on the Yankee staff felt that the game might be passing Joe by. More and more, computer statistics were being used to determine each day's lineup. Joe was one who preferred his memory and his discussions with his coaching staff. After four straight seasons of no World Series, though, his way of doing things wasn't pleasing his bosses.

In a shocking move following 2007, the Yankees chose to offer him a smaller contract, and his pride made him turn it down. He went to Florida, where the Steinbrenners had their offices, and said he didn't think he deserved a pay cut.

By not taking their offer, he was resigning. He could have stayed, but it was clear that the owners wanted a change and were relieved by his decision. They debated whether to hire Don Mattingly, who had come back as a coach, or Joe Girardi, and they chose Girardi, who loved his notebooks filled with statistical reports. Joe had managed the Marlins for a season—successfully—and seemed to have what it took. Torre and Mattingly both wound up managing the Los Angeles Dodgers, one after the other.

CHAPTER 55

Good-bye, Ol' Yankee Stadium

In Girardi's first season as manager, 2008, the Yankees failed to make the postseason for the first time since 1993, not including the strike year of '94 in which they were in first place when the season ended. Mike Mussina won twenty games for the first time in his career in 2008, but like Jason Giambi, his time with the Yankees produced no world championships. And then he retired.

And yet, there was something good about not winning, because 2008 was the last year of "old" Yankee Stadium, and without playing in October, fans could be sure that the last game of the regular season was, in fact, the last game there. So the ceremonies took on special meaning because they knew this was it.

The team celebrated the final year all season long, with special guests pulling a lever each game to mark the countdown on the scoreboard. When the countdown got to zero, the scoreboard read FOREVER.

And so on that final night at "the House that Ruth Built," playing against the Orioles, Babe's daughter Julia threw out the ceremonial first pitch, the 1922 American League pennant was displayed in the bleachers, and great Yankees of the past were called onto the field to stand at their old positions, along with the children of Munson, Martin, Maris, Mantle, and Murcer, and the widows of Rizzuto and Hunter. Ellie Howard's daughter was there. There were big cheers for Bernie Williams, in his first time back to the stadium since he'd reluctantly retired after 2006. The cheers were special for the Murcer family; Bobby had died that very summer. The greatest cheers were for Yogi Berra, who since DiMaggio's passing had been considered the "greatest living Yankee." But out they all came, Reggie Jackson to cheers of "REG-GIE!" and Paul O'Neill to "PAUL O-NEILL," and there were Winfield, Randolph, Richardson, Michael, Nettles, Boggs, Chambliss, Skowron, Ford, Larsen, Wells, Cone, Gossage, Guidry—what a night in the old ballpark.

Girardi pulled Jeter from shortstop while the ninth inning was being played so that Derek could have his own ovation. It was a nice dramatic moment for the full house.

Mariano Rivera came in to pitch the final inning and retired Brian Roberts on a ground out to end the game, with the Yankees winning 7–3 and catcher Jose Molina hitting the last home run. Babe Ruth, of course, had hit the first.

No one left their seats. The team gathered on the field, and the captain, Jeter, spoke to the fans, saying, "We're relying on you to take the memories from this stadium, add them to the new memories to come at the new Yankee Stadium, and continue to pass them on from generation to generation."

Jeter had not shown much sentiment earlier in his career, but he had grown into it. His parents had reminded him to "make sure you enjoy this." And he did.

Frank Sinatra's "New York, New York" played over and over until the ballpark finally emptied for the last time, well past midnight.

Yankee Stadium, "the House That Ruth Built," was history.

CHAPTER 56

In with the New!

The new ballpark, built just across the street, was big enough to fit the old one into—but it had more luxury suites and a smaller seating capacity. The team would no longer be able to draw four million fans a year. There were a lot of shops and food stands, but the most important test was passed—once you were inside, you felt like you were still in Yankee Stadium. The famous facade design, which had dropped down from the roof in the original stadium, was restored in the new one.

Everything about the new park was the latest and the greatest. The scoreboard was so big and so high-def that fans often found themselves watching the video more than the live game.

To beef up the 2009 team, the Yankees signed first baseman Mark Teixeira to replace Giambi; outfielder Nick Swisher, a personable crowd pleaser; and pitchers CC Sabathia and A. J. Burnett as starters. Sabathia, already an established star from his days in Cleveland, would eventually be tied for the most wins in the majors among active pitchers once Pettitte retired. And there was a lot of weight behind his billowing uniform—he weighed over three hundred pounds!

The old Yankee Stadium site became home to sandlot baseball fields in 2010. (Marty Appel Collection)

They joined a team that had signed Johnny Damon in 2006, a rare move of a very popular Red Sox player to New York. (Others over the years had been Ruth, Ruffing, Luis Tiant, Boggs, and later Jacoby Ellsbury in 2014.) The Red Sox fans—also known as Red Sox Nation—almost always felt betrayed when they lost one of their players to the Yankees through free agency.

Missing on opening day was Alex Rodriguez. He was recovering from surgery on his right hip, but he had also been revealed to have been caught using steroids during the time when the test results were supposed to be secret. He had been a Yankee at the time. Someone had leaked the results, and *Sports Illustrated* reported them. There would be no suspension for A-Rod, because those tests weren't covered by the current Joint Drug Agreement, but it was now clear that he was a user.

Opening day at the new stadium once again made Yankee fans feel great about their history. Yogi threw out the first pitch. Bernie Williams played "Take

Me Out to the Ballgame" on his guitar, while John Fogerty played his song "Centerfield." Kelly Clarkson sang the national anthem.

The two starting pitchers were Sabathia and Cliff Lee for Cleveland. This would prove to be ironic, because when the World Series came along, Lee had been traded to Philadelphia, and again it would be Sabathia and Lee in game one of the Series!

To get to the Series, the Yankees won 103 games and then beat the Twins and the Angels in the postseason play-offs. There were great milestones along the way—Damon getting the first hit in the new stadium, Posada the first home run. A-Rod returned on May 8 and homered his first time up. Rivera got his five hundredth career save, and Jeter passed Lou Gehrig for most hits as a Yankee. Derek would go on to bat .334, win a Gold Glove, and finish third in MVP voting. (It was one award he was never able to win.)

Fifteen times, the 2009 Yankees won a game in walk-off fashion on their last at bat, and A. J. Burnett made it a tradition to hit the hero with a shaving-cream pie in the face, usually while he was being interviewed on TV.

Joe Girardi wore number 27 during the season as the Yankees sought their twenty-seventh world championship. Would it work?

By finding themselves in the World Series, it certainly might. The new faces had come through, and in the postseason, no one swung a bigger bat than A-Rod, who batted .455 against the Twins and .429 against the Angels. In the World Series, he drove in six more runs. The hero, however, was Hideki Matsui, who won the MVP award, batted .615, and slugged a big pinch-hit home run in game three. It took six games for the Yankees to claim their twenty-seventh world championship (Girardi switched to number 28 the following year), and they were back on top for the first time since 2000.

Sadly, baseball being a business, Matsui and Damon both left via free agency after the season, and these two very popular players moved on. Matsui was so well loved that in 2013 he signed a "one-day contract" with New York so that he could retire as a Yankee, and the team honored him with a Hideki Matsui Day.

The new Yankee Stadium on opening day, 2009. (Marty Appel Collection)

Much was made of the Core Four—Pettitte, Jeter, Rivera, and Posada—who had now won five world championships together since they broke in together in 1995. Jeter, Rivera, and Posada played seventeen years together—no three players had ever done that before. In fairness, Bernie Williams was a fifth member of this small and beloved group, but he started earlier and retired earlier than they did. Still, they were all important to the first four of those five championships in creating a modern era for the Yankees dynasty.

CHAPTER 57

Sheppard, Steinbrenner Pass

In 2010 the Yankees' longtime public address announcer, Bob Sheppard, died at age ninety-nine. He hadn't done the PA announcing since 2007, but he was still known as the "Voice of Yankee Stadium."

Just two days later, the man most responsible for the new stadium died. George Steinbrenner, "the Boss," who owned the team for thirty-seven years, and whose teams won eleven pennants and seven world championships, died of a heart attack in Tampa at the age of eighty. Many felt the new ballpark was, in fact, "the House That George Built."

Statues of Steinbrenner would be erected at Yankee Stadium and at Steinbrenner Field at the spring training field in Tampa. An enormous plaque was dedicated in his memory in Monument Park at Yankee Stadium. Mariano Rivera placed roses at home plate before the first home game after Sheppard's and Steinbrenner's passings, in honor of them both, and Jeter addressed the crowd and spoke of them as well.

On the day Steinbrenner died, the Yankees were defending world champions and sitting in first place. It would have made him proud.

Management of the team fell to his four children, mostly his youngest son, Hal, along with team president Randy Levine, chief operating officer Lonn Trost, and general manager Brian Cashman. For a while, the children spoke of getting the payroll down so that the team would not have to pay a "luxury tax" on top of all the high salaries, but when they recognized the need to spend a lot to stay competitive, they relaxed their feelings on that.

More than anything, the team continued to be known for putting its profits back into the team to continue to improve and to bring in big stars. Other owners were accused of pocketing the profits their teams had made. Not so for the Yankees.

The 2010 Yankees couldn't hold on to first place. They captured the wild card, but were knocked out by Minnesota in the first round. Girardi would have to continue to wear number 28.

The years 2011 and 2012 also fell short, when Detroit stopped the Yankee hitters cold in the postseason. A lot of fans were screaming at certain hitters for their failures to come through—forgetting that when no one is hitting, it is probably the good pitching on the other side that is responsible. Baseball people have always believed that good pitching stops good hitting, not the other way around. And in those two play-offs, the Tigers just had great pitching.

The Yankee stars were starting to get old. The story is as old as baseball. They needed young players to come along and take their places, but that is not always easy.

CHAPTER 58

Milestones and Retirements

On July 9, 2011, Derek Jeter became the first Yankee ever to record three thousand hits, and he did it in a big way, hitting a home run for number three thousand and going five-for-five that afternoon in Yankee Stadium. People had been waiting with great anticipation for that three thousandth, but no one expected five hits in one day to put him over the top. Jeter also passed Mickey Mantle that season for most games played as a Yankee, while Mariano Rivera passed Trevor Hoffman for most lifetime saves, and also became the first man to ever pitch in one thousand games for one team.

Posada retired after 2011, but he got a pinch-hit single that year to win the game that clinched the Eastern Division title—and gave the fans a chance to roar, "Hip Hip Jorge!" one more time.

Rivera missed most of the 2012 season when he tore a ligament in his leg, suffered while fielding fly balls during batting practice in Kansas City. It was the last year of his contract, but he did not want it to end with the sight of him being driven off on a groundskeeper's cart, unable to walk. He came back in 2013—one last round—and was as good as he had ever been.

That year turned into a yearlong Mariano celebration. Teams in all the cities in which the Yankees played honored him, and he, in turn, met with special fans or special club employees at each stop.

He was the last player to wear number 42, since baseball had retired that number in honor of Jackie Robinson back in 1997. Players wearing it were allowed to keep wearing it, and Mariano would be the last. His Yankee 42 was officially retired on Mariano Rivera Day at Yankee Stadium on September 22, 2013 (Mrs. Jackie Robinson was on hand), and he spoke to the crowd, surrounded by old teammates like O'Neill, Tino Martinez, Matsui, Williams, Posada, and Joe Torre, too. And he came in to pitch that day, as always, to the sounds of Metallica's "Enter Sandman," which had become his theme.

But the best was still to come, four days later. There were no ceremonies on that day, but it would be his final appearance in Yankee Stadium—the team did

Mariano Rivera was honored on his retirement day in 2013, and even the Tampa Bay Rays stood by their dugout to watch the ceremonies. (Marty Appel Collection)

not qualify for the postseason. This time he came in during the eighth inning, as cell-phone cameras from the full house flashed. It was his last appearance on the mound. And with two out, Girardi sent Jeter and Pettitte to the mound to relieve him, so that he could savor the applause one last time.

"Time to go," said Jeter as the two old teammates approached. Mariano, in tears, hugged Pettitte (who would also retire that week) and walked off with his pals.

For Jeter it had been a rough year, and the smile on his face was good to see. After a sensational season in 2012, he had broken his ankle in the postseason against Detroit and broken it again during rehabilitation work. The 2013 season was pretty much a lost season for him—he played only seventeen games, during a year in which the Yankees used fifty-six players, many of them clearly not ready for the major leagues yet.

Derek then announced that 2014 would be his final season. No one had ever spent more seasons with the Yankees than he did (twenty), played as many games, or represented the team better.

After the season ended, the Yankees saw Cano leave as a free agent, after nine seasons with the Yanks. Cano left to take a huge contract offer from Seattle, negotiated by his agent, singer Jay-Z. It broke the hearts of Yankee fans, but as Brian Cashman said, "We had done to us what we've been doing to others for a long time."

Meanwhile, the team waited out a ruling on Alex Rodriguez, who had been caught once again using performance-enhancing drugs. An arbitrator ruled that he would be suspended for the full 2014 season. The Yankees wouldn't have to pay him while he was out, which they considered a break, since he had now had two hip surgeries and just wasn't the player he had once been.

With the money saved on Rodriguez's salary, and feeling the need to spend big to stay pennant-ready, the Yankees gave big contracts for 2014 to Carlos Beltran, Jacoby Ellsbury, Brian McCann, and Japanese pitcher Masahiro Tanaka, who had gone 24–0 in Japan in 2013.

While injuries crippled the Yankees pitching in 2014, with even Tanaka going down after proving to be a sensation, Girardi managed to guide them to a second-place finish in the American League East. It wasn't enough to get them into the play-offs, and it was the first time since the early 1990s that they missed two years in a row.

But much of the 2014 season was about the farewell year for Jeter, who concluded twenty seasons without ever playing one inning in the field other than at shortstop. In his whole career, he played only 4 games (out of 2,747), in which the Yankees had been eliminated from play-off hopes.

In his final game in Yankee Stadium, he drove in the winning run with a ninth-inning single, and then bowed out for good three days later in Boston, leaving with 3,465 hits—sixth on the all-time list. Most remarkable perhaps were the 200 hits he got in postseason play, covering 158 games, all against top-flight teams.

But Jeter was always about team play, and he would say that being on five world championship clubs topped any individual accomplishment he may have had.

The Yankees continued as the most successful sports franchise in all American sports, and always there with big personalities, big stars, big hopes, loyal fans, and breaking news.

The Pride of the Yankees, the old movie about Lou Gehrig, was still in force.

CHAPTER 59

Keeping the Tradition Alive

The Yankees have always stood for excellence and have always managed to find big-name players to carry on their traditions. They have always been fortunate to have wealthy owners who could put profits into signing big stars, and they were smart enough to take advantage of doing business in New York, where they could make more money than other teams.

Those who rooted against the Yankees generally did so for that very reason. They thought it was an unfair advantage to have the most money and to be able to win because of it.

But it takes more than money. It takes good managers, dedicated players, and a dedicated front-office staff where everyone contributes in his or her own way. And the loyal fans didn't hurt—playing at home before adoring crowds was always a boost to the players.

From Ruth to Gehrig to DiMaggio to Berra to Mantle to Munson to Jackson to Winfield to Mattingly to Jeter, the Yankees have been a team that always managed to find the right guy. There have been dry patches, there have been times when a lot of fans stayed home, but in the end, they always seemed to deliver.

Many retired players have said, "I'd give three years of my career to have spent one year with the Yankees, for all that means after you retire." And it's true—fans remember their Yankees, and being a Yankee stays with a player for life.

Players come and go, even owners come and go, but the fans are forever.

Appendix

Yankees Selected for All-Star Teams

The All-Star Game was first played in 1933, and the Yankees have had the most players selected. The following is the full roster of Yankee All-Stars, sorted by the number of years in which they were selected.

16

Mickey Mantle

15

Yogi Berra

14

Derek Jeter

13

Joe DiMaggio, Mariano Rivera

11

Bill Dickey

9

Elston Howard

8

Whitey Ford, Dave Winfield

7

Lou Gehrig, Joe Gordon, Bobby Richardson, Alex Rodriguez

6

Lefty Gomez, Red Ruffing, Charlie Keller, Thurman Munson, Don Mattingly

5

Tommy Henrich, Phil Rizzuto, Allie Reynolds, Gil McDougald, Bill Skowron, Mel Stottlemyre, Graig Nettles, Willie Randolph, Reggie Jackson, Bernie Williams, Jorge Posada, Robinson Cano

4

Red Rolfe, Spud Chandler, Vic Raschi, Bobby Murcer, Goose Gossage, Ron Guidry, Rickey Henderson, Wade Boggs, Paul O'Neill

3

Ben Chapman, George Selkirk, Joe Page, Hank Bauer, Tony Kubek, Roger Maris, Joe Pepitone, Sparky Lyle, Tommy John, Andy Pettitte, Jason Giambi, CC Sabathia

2

Babe Ruth, Frank Crosetti, Monte Pearson, Johnny Murphy, Hank Borowy, Ernie Bonham, George McQuinn, Bob Turley, Ryne Duren, Tom Tresh, Catfish Hunter, Dave Righetti, Steve Sax, Jimmy Key, David Cone, Roger Clemens, Alfonso Soriano, Hideki Matsui, Gary Sheffield, Curtis Granderson

1

Tony Lazzeri, Marius Russo, Johnny Lindell, Buddy Rosar, Rollie Hemsley, George Stirnweiss, Billy Johnson, Aaron Robinson, Spec Shea, Tommy Byrne, Jerry Coleman, Ed Lopat, Johnny Mize, Johnny Sain, Irv Noren, Johnny Kucks, Billy Martin, Bob Grim, Bobby Shantz, Jim Coates, Luis Arroyo, Ralph Terry, Jim Bouton, Al Downing, Fritz Peterson, Roy White, Bobby Bonds, Chris Chambliss, Mickey Rivers, Bucky Dent, Ron Davis, Phil Niekro, Scott

Sanderson, Roberto Kelly, Mike Stanley, John Wetteland, Tino Martinez, Scott Brosius, David Wells, Mike Stanton, Robin Ventura, Tom Gordon, Javier Vasquez, Mark Teixeira, Phil Hughes, Nick Swisher, Russell Martin, David Robertson, Masahiro Tanaka, Dellin Betances

Yankees Who Won MVP Award

Mickey Mantle (3), Yogi Berra (3), Joe DiMaggio (3), Lou Gehrig (2), Alex Rodriguez (2), Roger Maris (2), Babe Ruth, Joe Gordon, Phil Rizzuto, Elston Howard, Thurman Munson, Don Mattingly (1 each)

Yankees Who Won Cy Young Award

Bob Turley, Whitey Ford, Sparky Lyle, Ron Guidry, Roger Clemens

Yankees Who Won Rookie of the Year Award

Gil McDougald, Bob Grim, Tony Kubek, Tom Tresh, Stan Bahnsen, Thurman Munson, Dave Righetti, Derek Jeter

Yankees Who Won Gold Glove Awards

Don Mattingly (9), Bernie Williams (6), Bobby Richardson (5), Ron Guidry (5), Dave Winfield (5), Derek Jeter (5), Bobby Shantz (4), Mark Teixeira (3), Mike Mussina (3), Thurman Munson (3), Joe Pepitone (3), Elston Howard (2), Robinson Cano (2), Graig Nettles (2), Wade Boggs (2), Chris Chambliss, Scott Brosius, Norm Siebern, Roger Maris, Mickey Mantle, Tom Tresh, Bobby Murcer (1 each)

Yankees Who Won Batting Championships

Joe DiMaggio (2), Babe Ruth, Lou Gehrig, George Stirnweiss, Mickey Mantle, Don Mattingly, Paul O'Neill, Bernie Williams (1 each)

Yankees Who Won Home Run Championships

Babe Ruth (10), Mickey Mantle (4), Lou Gehrig (3), Joe DiMaggio (2), Wally

Pipp (2), Alex Rodriguez (2), Nick Etten, Bob Meusel, Roger Maris, Graig Nettles, Reggie Jackson, Mark Teixeira (1 each)

Yankees Who Won RBI Championships

Lou Gehrig (5), Babe Ruth (4), Joe DiMaggio (2), Roger Maris (2), Bob Meusel, Nick Etten, Mickey Mantle, Don Mattingly, Alex Rodriguez, Mark Teixeira, Curtis Granderson (1 each)

Yankees World Championships

1923, 1927, 1928, 1932, 1936, 1937, 1938, 1939, 1941, 1943, 1947, 1949, 1950, 1951, 1952, 1953, 1956, 1958, 1961, 1962, 1977, 1978, 1996, 1998, 1999, 2000, 2009

Yankees American League Championships

1921, 1922, 1923, 1926, 1927, 1928, 1932, 1936, 1937, 1938, 1939, 1941, 1942, 1943, 1947, 1949, 1950, 1951, 1952, 1953, 1955, 1956, 1957, 1958, 1960, 1961, 1962, 1963, 1964, 1976, 1977, 1978, 1981, 1996, 1998, 1999, 2000, 2001, 2003, 2009

Yankees American League Eastern Division Championships (Division Play Began 1969)

1976, 1977, 1978, 1980, 1981, 1995, 1996, 1998, 1999, 2000, 2001, 2002, 2003, 2004, 2005, 2006, 2009, 2011, 2012

Yankees in the Hall of Fame (Significant Achievements Came as Yankees)

Home Run Baker, Ed Barrow, Yogi Berra, Wade Boggs, Jack Chesbro, Earle Combs, Bill Dickey, Joe DiMaggio, Whitey Ford, Lou Gehrig, Lefty Gomez, Joe Gordon, Goose Gossage, Clark Griffith, Bucky Harris, Rickey Henderson, Waite Hoyt, Miller Huggins, Catfish Hunter, Reggie Jackson, Willie Keeler, Tony Lazzeri, Larry MacPhail, Lee MacPhail, Mickey Mantle, Joe McCarthy,

Johnny Mize, Herb Pennock, Phil Rizzuto, Red Ruffing, Jacob Ruppert, Babe Ruth, Joe Sewell, Enos Slaughter, Casey Stengel, Joe Torre, George Weiss, Dave Winfield

Yankees Retired Numbers

1 (Billy Martin), 2 (Derek Jeter), 3 (Babe Ruth), 4 (Lou Gehrig), 5 (Joe DiMaggio), 6 (Joe Torre), 7 (Mickey Mantle), 8 (Bill Dickey and Yogi Berra), 9 (Roger Maris), 10 (Phil Rizzuto), 15 (Thurman Munson), 16 (Whitey Ford), 23 (Don Mattingly), 32 (Elston Howard), 37 (Casey Stengel), 42 (Mariano Rivera), 44 (Reggie Jackson), 49 (Ron Guidry)

Suggested Reading

Appel, Marty. *Pinstripe Empire: The New York Yankees from Before the Babe to After the Boss.* New York: Bloomsbury, 2012.

———. *162–0.* Chicago: Triumph, 2010.

———. *Now Pitching for the Yankees: Spinning the News for Mickey, George and Billy.* Kingston, NY: Total Sports, 2001.

Carrieri, Joe, as told to Zander Hollander. *Yankee Batboy.* New York: Prentice-Hall, 1955.

Creamer, Robert. *Babe: The Legend Comes to Life.* New York: Simon & Schuster, 1974.

DiMaggio, Joe. *Lucky to Be a Yankee.* Revised edition. New York: Grosset & Dunlap, 1957.

Graham, Frank. *The New York Yankees: An Informal History.* New York: G.P. Putnam's Sons, 1943.

Honig, Donald. *The New York Yankees.* Revised edition. New York: Crown, 1987.

Howard, Arlene, with Ralph Wimbish. *Elston and Me: The Story of the First Black Yankee.* Columbia: University of Missouri Press, 2001.

Mantle, Merlyn, Mickey Mantle Jr., David Mantle, and Dan Mantle, with Mickey Herskowitz. *A Hero All His Life: A Memoir by the Mantle Family*. New York: HarperCollins, 1996.

McCough, Matthew. *Bat Boy: My True Life Adventures Coming of Age with the New York Yankees*. New York: Doubleday, 2005.

New York Yankees Media Relations Department. *Media Guides (annual)*. Bronx, NY: New York Yankees.

Olney, Buster. *The Last Night of the Yankee Dynasty*. New York: Ecco, 2004.

Pepe, Phil. *The Yankees: The Authorized History of the New York Yankees*. Dallas: Taylor, 1995.

Poekel, Charie. *Babe & the Kid*. Charleston, SC: The History Press, 2007.

Prudenti, Frank. *Memories of a Yankee Batboy, 1956–1961*. Bronx, NY: Pru Publications, 2003.

Ritter, Lawrence. *The Glory of Their Times*. New York: Macmillan, 1966.

Robinson, Ray. *Iron Horse*. New York: Norton, 1990.

Santasiere III, Al, and Mark Vancil. *The Final Season: The Official Retrospective*. New York: Rare Air, 2008.

Stout, Glenn, and Richard A. Johnson. *Yankees Century*. Boston: Houghton Mifflin, 2002.

Swearingen, Randall. *A Great Teammate: The Legend of Mickey Mantle*. Champaign, IL: Sports Publishing, 2007.

Vaccaro, Mike. *Emperors and Idiots*. New York: Doubleday, 2005.

Vancil, Mark, and Mark Mandrake. *One Hundred Years: New York Yankees: The Official Retrospective*. New York: Ballantine, 2002.

Vancil, Mark, and Al Santasiere III. *Yankee Stadium: The Official Retrospective*. New York: Pocket Books, 2008.

Index